NICOLAS HELLER

with JASON DIAMOND

PHOTOGRAPHS BY JEREMY COHEN

DEYST.
An Imprint of WILLIAM MORROW

FOR
MOM, DAD, NAOMI, AND TOBY

CONTENTS

THE BRONX

STATEN ISLAND

INTRODUCTION

ew York City means something different to everybody. For me, it's people like Yuval Dekel at Liebman's Deli, who took over for his dad and kept the last kosher deli in the Bronx thriving. It's Gavin Hussey serving jerk chicken that he'd feel as comfortable making for people from his native Jamaica as he is for Brooklynites. It's Demetri Siafakas standing behind the counter talking to customers at Peter Pan Donuts, Julia Wijesinghe serving Sri Lankan food and culture to anybody who will take the ferry to Staten Island, and Big Mike and the dozens of barbers who speak Italian, Russian, Greek, Spanish, French, Polish, Uzbek, and Farsi at Astor Place Hairstylists.

Even though I'm known as the unofficial talent scout of New York City, I never realized how lucky I was to be born and raised here until I left. Manhattan was all I ever knew, and at some point, I thought I wanted something else. After college, I followed in the footsteps of countless other New Yorkers who thought their fortunes would be better out West, and I moved to Los Angeles. My goal was to make it as a music video director. What I discovered was the whole thing about how the grass is always greener on the other side, but I don't know much about grass—I grew up around Union Square.

I got to Los Angeles, and, after six short months, I was miserable. I couldn't book work or find a decent slice. I failed my driving test three times. It just wasn't doing it for me. I was all ready to get stuck in that rut so many twentysomethings get into when their big ideas don't pan out.

When I came back to NYC, I wound up finding inspiration where I should have been looking all along—home. I had gotten a little more perspective, and instead of just Manhattan, I began exploring the city as a whole, meeting people from all over, learning about who they were, where they came from, and what motivated them to do something that stood out in a city of millions. In 2013, I started a web series called *No Your City*. The first episode featured Te'Devan, a local fixture people knew as "The 6'7" Jew Who Will Rap for You," as the sign he carried advertised.

Why would I need to go anywhere else in the world when I live in a place with literally millions of unique individuals, each with their own story? You step out the door and maybe you see a guy riding a bike while balancing a trash can on his head, then you get on the subway and it's a dancer yelling "SHOWTIME," or a mariachi band is playing. Maybe the guy handing you a buttered roll has a beautiful singing voice, or maybe you walk past a basketball court and see a teenage girl schooling a group of guys like she's Jalen Brunson. New Yorkers are characters, whether they're trying to be or not.

I started making new friends: the walking work of art that is the Green Lady of Brooklyn, the greatest living street golfer Tiger Hood, BigTime Tommie, Wayne Diamond, Cugine, and many more. Some of them I met because I just happened to be hanging out at Anthony & Son Panini Shoppe in Williamsburg, where a few of them are regulars. Others I might have been introduced to because they had some exceptional talent. More than a few I just saw walking down the street. I started posting about them on my accounts, and while people loved the characters in my universe, the response to the business owners and unique spots all over the city was often just as big, and sometimes bigger.

Then the COVID-19 pandemic happened. New York City had it bad. The city shut down. The streets were empty. Tourists were gone. New York has been counted out so many times before, but time after time, we've come back. The *Daily News* "Ford to City: Drop Dead" headline era of the 1970s, the gritty 1980s, 9/11, and however many other ups and downs you can count, New York has weathered everything. But the pandemic was something else. Along with the death toll, hospitals filling up, and people leaving, businesses were closing left and right. The only thing I figured I could do was make videos of owners trying to keep the lights on, and also share information on how to help them and other New Yorkers who were struggling to get through one of the scariest times any of us can recall. Fortunately, we were able to make an impact and raise enough money and garner enough support to help keep many businesses afloat.

Once things started to reopen, I found myself in a unique position as someone with New York in their name. Everyone wanted to know my favorite places in the city. They had questions: where to get a good bialy, if the pizza at this place or that was worth trying or not, and where to find the best selection of jazz on vinyl. Some things I could answer, others I had to investigate. Eventually, I figured there had to be a better way.

This book is basically one big answer: 100 go-to spots across all five boroughs. This is not just a guidebook: This is a document of a moment in New York City.

It's a moment of transition. What does the future hold? I have no idea. But I'm hopeful that these small businesses will always have a place here, and that in twenty, fifty, or one hundred years when somebody walks into a bookstore and sees a copy of this book, they'll open it up and find that all the places we went to are still in business.

There are hundreds of other businesses I could have included in this book. To make it a little easier, I didn't get too deep into bars, cafés, and fine-dining establishments, etc. I love those places, but the fact is that I don't spend a lot of time in bars; I'm more of a plate-of-eggs-at-a-diner guy than a cloth-napkin one.

Believe me, it was hard to get this list down to 100, but it felt like a good benchmark. Some are places I've been going to my entire life, others I discovered during the pandemic, and some recs were suggested to me by friends who know certain neighborhoods and communities better than I do. Either way, my hope is that the choices, in some small way,

represent this beautiful city that is my home.

To me, it doesn't matter if you're from out of town or a born-and-raised local. This book is for everybody, the same way the city I care so deeply about is open to all who show it love and appreciation. I hope you'll check out as many places as you can. When you do, be sure to talk up the owners and employees. Learn what makes them get up every morning and keep going despite the train delays, random people yelling, weird smells, high prices, and everything else this city throws their way. If you do, I promise you'll start to understand what it took me twenty-three years to figure out: New York City is a million things, a million businesses, and more than 8 million people. All of them have their own unique stories, and it all comes together to make my home a world unto itself.

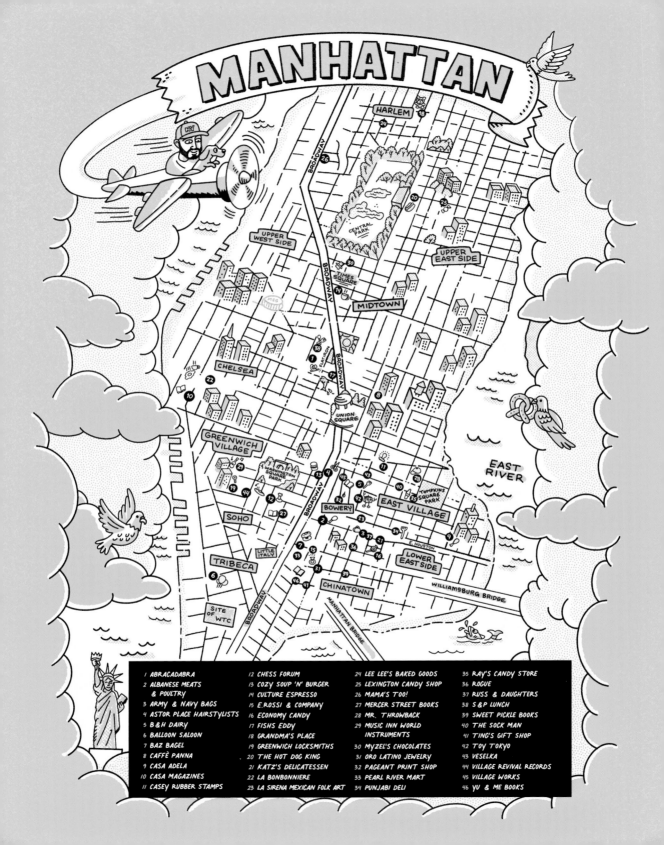

MANHATTAN

1 ABRACADABRA
2 ALBANESE MEATS & POULTRY
3 ARMY & NAVY BAGS
4 ASTOR PLACE HAIRSTYLISTS
5 B & H DAIRY
6 BALLOON SALOON
7 BAZ BAGEL
8 CAFFÈ PANNA
9 CASA ADELA
10 CASA MAGAZINES
11 CASEY RUBBER STAMPS
12 CHESS FORUM
13 COZY SOUP 'N' BURGER
14 CULTURE ESPRESSO
15 E. ROSSI & COMPANY
16 ECONOMY CANDY
17 FISHS EDDY
18 GRANDMA'S PLACE
19 GREENWICH LOCKSMITHS
20 THE HOT DOG KING
21 KATZ'S DELICATESSEN
22 LA BONBONNIERE
23 LA SIRENA MEXICAN FOLK ART
24 LEE LEE'S BAKED GOODS
25 LEXINGTON CANDY SHOP
26 MAMA'S TOO!
27 MERCER STREET BOOKS
28 MR. THROWBACK
29 MUSIC INN WORLD INSTRUMENTS
30 MYZEL'S CHOCOLATES
31 ORO LATINO JEWELRY
32 PAGEANT PRINT SHOP
33 PEARL RIVER MART
34 PUNJABI DELI
35 RAY'S CANDY STORE
36 ROGUE
37 RUSS & DAUGHTERS
38 S & P LUNCH
39 SWEET PICKLE BOOKS
40 THE SOCK MAN
41 TING'S GIFT SHOP
42 TOY TOKYO
43 VESELKA
44 VILLAGE REVIVAL RECORDS
45 VILLAGE WORKS
46 YU & ME BOOKS

There's a reason locals call Manhattan "the City." You have nearly 1.7 million people residing here, and that doesn't even begin to count the nonresidents who are there on any given day, from tourists to commuters from New Jersey, Pennsylvania, or Connecticut. I get how it can seem chaotic to outsiders. There's constantly a jackhammer pounding in the distance and car horns blaring, and you can't go more than a block or two without seeing scaffolding covering a building.

Since I was born and raised in Manhattan, it's normal to me. Some people love it and thrive off the energy, but I can understand how not everybody gets the city. From 1785 to 1790, Manhattan was the capital of the United States, but I think the Founding Fathers were pioneers at recognizing that New York City isn't a town for everyone. Today, Manhattan is New York City's center of finance, media, entertainment, and government. This by default makes it a kind of unofficial capital of the country, and arguably the world.

Some people don't love it when New Yorkers say that, but I don't make the rules.

Whether you've lived in Manhattan your whole life or are in town for the weekend, there's always something new to see. It could be somebody creating art on the sidewalk, but it could also be something simple, like the beauty of an old building up in Washington Heights that you'd never noticed, or somebody dancing in the Washington Square Park fountain. A lot of my picks in this book are in Manhattan for the simple reason that I'm from there and I spend a lot of my time there.

Manhattan is where the Harlem Renaissance, Beat Generation, and punk rock all happened. It's hot dogs in front of the Metropolitan Museum of Art, halal chicken and rice before going into MoMA, bagels and lox on the Lower East Side. It's always changing, but somehow stays the same, with its frantic pace, smells, sights, and sounds. Manhattan is what people usually mean when they say the City, and it will always be that way. It truly has everything you could ever want.

ABRACADABRA

19 WEST 21ST STREET

Does New York City have everything? It's impossible to say. You can get cuisine from nearly anywhere on the globe, rubber stamps in the East Village, basically any magazine you can hope for at Casa, cookbooks or mystery novels at stores strictly dedicated to those genres, vintage shops galore, and just about anything else you can think of. But what if it's the middle of April and you really need a Billy the Puppet mask from the Saw film franchise?

That's where Abracadabra comes in. You want masks, fake blood, one of those old hand buzzers, whatever, they've got it 365 days a year. But it's during October when the place really becomes one of the most popular spots in the entire city. Abracadabra is Halloween central.

It's rare you'll hear somebody call something in New York City "underrated," but people really do overlook our love for Halloween. Just the annual Village Halloween Parade and the days leading up to October 31, when hundreds of dogs dress up for their special costume party in Tompkins Square Park, should be enough to make NYC a Halloween destination. And we've got a temple of all things spooky and fun in Abracadabra. Thanks to the three floors of masks, wigs, costumes, and magic tricks, there's usually a line out the door before everybody goes out on October 31. But being open year-round means Abracadabra has turned into a local institution, not just some weird Spirit Halloween operation that opens at the start of fall and closes well before Thanksgiving. It's a local business, and also a family one.

Originally opened by Paul Blum in 1981, the store was bought by Robert Pinzon and his brother, Joe, in 2007, then handed down to Robert's daughter, Janine, and her husband, Brian Clark. There are a lot

Make sure to stop by their magic section, where an in-house magician can teach you some tricks.

TIP

of family businesses in the city, but there's something really cool about imagining dinner conversations about what's new in the plastic vampire fang industry and some of the crazier things that come through the shop.

It's easy to forget, but people do need costumes year-round, for everything from parties to school plays. Then you look at all the magic tricks for sale as you walk in the door and remember there will always be a new generation of kids obsessed with telling you to pick a card and making coins disappear. But most of all, the film industry in New York is always in need of props and places to film. Abracadabra provides both. Production teams for institutions like *Saturday Night Live* and *Law & Order* regularly pop into Abracadabra when they need anything from fog machines to very real-looking fake skulls. They know to head to 19 West 21st.

I've been a customer since I was a little kid. It's easy to take this sort of merchandise for granted nowadays,

especially since you can buy anything online any time of the year. But I can't tell you how many times I wandered past or inside Abracadabra, and the kind of impact it's had on me. I love knowing it's there and how, even if it's the middle of July, it's fun to just go look at all the stuff, maybe buy a Michael Myers mask or a fake beard. You know, important stuff.

MANHATTAN

3

ALBANESE MEATS & POULTRY

238 ELIZABETH STREET

Jennifer Prezioso is a vital connection to Little Italy's past. The butcher shop she runs has been operating for over a century and is smack in the middle of one of Manhattan's trendiest neighborhoods. Jennifer's grandfather, the late Moe Albanese, known to locals as Moe the Butcher and to Jennifer as Grandpa Moe, was a neighborhood legend, but getting older made it hard for him to keep the business going. Jennifer, who is also an actor, started showing up to help out, not thinking that one day she'd be running the store. But she started learning the ropes, and soon she was behind the counter.

Back in the day, there used to be more than a few butchers in the neighborhood. But things changed, the Italian community started leaving, and many

TIP

The ribeye is sort of the signature cut here. It's where Moe came up with the store's tagline: "I got'cha steaks."

of the shop owners didn't have kids who wanted to take over. Moe was known as one of the best guys to get meat from in Manhattan, and it's almost like he held out, knowing that sooner or later somebody from his family would step in and take over.

Moe the Butcher passed away in 2020 at the age of ninety-five. For the community, it was a terrible loss. And Jennifer lost her grandfather as well as a friend and mentor. Keeping the shop running goes beyond a job; it's a tribute to the man who taught her so much. She thinks about the first thing he told her when she started trying to learn how to cut steaks. It's a good rule of thumb for meat, but also a smart way to look at life and how you treat others.

"I'd cut something and he'd look at it and go, 'Do you like that piece? If that was on your plate, would you eat it?' And I'd say 'No, I don't think so,' so he'd tell me to try again."

ARMY & NAVY BAGS

177 EAST HOUSTON STREET #2

In 2015, my friend told me he was going to take me to one of his spots. His main obsession is pins, and he says Army & Navy Bags is one of the best places to get them. I'd passed by before and never thought much of the place, but as soon as I walked in and met Henry, I knew I'd met somebody special. Anybody who has gone into NYC mom-and-pop shops knows it can take some time for the owners to warm up to you, but Henry truly treats everybody like a friend, and he's amassed a devoted following because of it.

If you're looking for anything camouflage, or an olive-colored coat, Army & Navy Bags is the first place I'll tell a person to check out. Henry knows everything, and his prices are some of the most reasonable in the city. His shop is crammed with everything from olive-green backpacks to wallets and parkas. I've taken everybody I know there, from Post Malone to Central Cee to benny blanco. Everybody buys something. "Besides the Statue of Liberty, they come to see me first!" Henry says with so much surprise and wonder. He doesn't understand how he's become not just a local favorite, but also a living landmark. He's a humble guy who shows up to work every day and treats everyone like

an honored guest whether they're famous or just somebody who needs a new army jacket, so the taste of fame is still strange to him: "Even my son said he saw me on Instagram!"

His prices are low, but if you're just looking for a boost of good energy, Henry won't charge you for that. In fact, I think in his downtime he recharges himself for the people who come in. The chances of walking in on Henry taking a nap on a pile of canvas army bags is about 50 percent. "Sometimes it's a little boring and I fall asleep," he told me once with a laugh.

When I asked him if he knew how much people loved his store, Henry shook his head. He's never really gotten a chance to realize how many people care about him because he's been too busy talking to everyone who stops in. He starts with a "Hello," asks them how they're doing, and within a minute or two, it's like he's got half the customer's biography. Henry's ability to make friends with anybody he meets is an art form unto itself.

To me, Henry embodies everything that's great about this city, and that's why whenever I'm nearby, I stop in. And the videos I post of my visits to his shop are always in the moment, one take, and real. Sometimes when I walk in, he's just chilling and it's totally natural.

Henry's fame has gone worldwide. People take pictures and videos in his shop all the time, and when they do, they always get the same reactions I see on my Instagram when I post about him: 100 percent positive. In a world filled with negativity, it seems that a New York City shop owner is the one thing we seem to all agree is good.

ASTOR PLACE HAIRSTYLISTS

740 BROADWAY, 2 ASTOR PLACE

 e lost a lot of good places during the COVID-19 pandemic, and my beloved barbershop, Astor Place Hairstylists, was nearly one of them. I just call it Astor Place. I've been descending the stairs into 740 Broadway since I was ten years old, and it's always been a vital place not just to me, but basically to everyone who has ever lived in and around the area. From Dave Chappelle and Macaulay Culkin to NBA stars, boxers, and politicians, everybody gets their hair cut, head shaved, beard trimmed, and everything in between at Astor Place.

And when I say I "descend," I really mean that. This local landmark is one of those spaces that really transports you to what seems like an entirely different world. It feels like this great big underground garage, so you have to take a second to get your bearings since natural light is basically nonexistent here. Once you collect yourself and remember you're still in Manhattan, your other senses start to take over. You look around and see chair after chair filled by customers being attended to by barbers. You smell all the various products in the air, and the sounds are like nothing you'll hear anywhere else. It's partially all the buzzing and snipping, but it's something else too: it's all the different kinds of talking you hear.

There's nothing like it when representing the cross section of humanity found in New York, maybe barring the subway. You get men, women, old, young, rich guys getting their hair cut next to NYU students and MTA bus drivers. And you've got half the globe represented. As the famous sign tells you when you walk down the stairs off the street and into the shop, there are over forty people working at any given time at Astor Place from Italy, Russia, Ukraine, Uzbekistan, the Dominican Republic, St. Lucia, Ecuador, Argentina, Venezuela, Brazil, Greece, Morocco, and, of course, New York City. Speak a language other than English, and it's likely somebody at Astor Place Hairstylists can talk to you.

Growing up, I didn't know any of the barbers by name. I was intimidated. The barbers didn't seem like they wanted to talk to a kid. A few years back, I noticed Astor Place following me on Instagram. I shot them a message and told them my story about how long I'd been a customer. They asked me to come in and introduce myself to everyone. So I started talking to people in the shop, getting their stories, learning about the different places they'd come from, and one day I popped my head into the storage area in the back, and that's where I first met Michael Saviello, aka Big Mike. He had his shirt off and was painting a Van Gogh–inspired Biggie Smalls. It blew me away.

A lot of cool people have worked at the barbershop since it opened in 1947, but Big Mike is a true legend. He was a manager for

over forty years, and when things looked like they were falling apart at Astor Place Hairstylists, a miracle happened: A handful of old customers who also came of age going downstairs for a cut, and who have since gone on to bigger and better things, all chipped in to save the place. Big Mike became a part owner, and things have been steadily getting better since. Not only that, but Big Mike's art is all over the walls, and

I made a short documentary about Big Mike and his painting career called *Big Mike Takes Lunch*. You can watch it online. Astor Place also has a lot of cool nightly events like comedy shows, sip and paints, and art shows. Follow them on Instagram to find out when things are happening.

TIP

PRICE LIST

• BUZZ CUT $30.00
• BLOW DRY 30 TO 40
• WASH CUT AND BLOW 35-45
• HI LITES (CAP) 75 UP
• HI LITES (FOIL) 95 UP
• SINGLE PROCESS 60 UP
• DOUBLE PROCESS 120 UP
• HOT SHAVE $30.00

he's become an art-world celebrity. People drop big cash for his paintings. But Big Mike is humble about it, and he's just happy to come to work every single day. "Honestly, down here it feels like not a lot has changed since I started, and I think that's part of what's so great about it," he tells me as his phone rings and his top muse, his wife, calls. "Hey, hon, let me call you back. I'm talking to Nico."

He hangs up and asks me if I need a haircut. At any other place, you're paying at least $65 for a cut and a beard trim. It's maybe half that at Astor when you factor in the tip you should always give your barber. I sit down in the chair, get my head shaved by my usual guy, Jeff, then go across the street to get a bite at Cozy Soup 'n' Burger (page 28).

MANHATTAN

B&H DAIRY

127 SECOND AVENUE

There are Jewish delis like Katz's that serve meat, and there *were* Jewish dairy restaurants that served fish and vegetarian fare, since kosher laws say you can't mix meat and milk. I say "were" because my friends James and Karla Murphy are pretty sure B&H Dairy is one of the last dairy spots, at least from that generation.

"It's been the same since we've been here," Karla says of the slim eatery. And I mean *slim*. It's a long lunch counter where New Yorkers sit shoulder to shoulder, but

that's the way things used to be, and New Yorkers don't seem to mind it today. B&H opened in 1938, and it's one of those places that contains a million little stories and has seen countless faces of everyone from immigrants to hippies, punks to poets. This is the East Village, after all.

Besides ownership, the place has seen very few changes in terms of what it serves and how it looks. In 2003, husband and wife Fawzy and Ola Abdelwahed took over the restaurant and have steered B&H through

every sort of disaster you can imagine, including a lethal gas explosion that literally took out a chunk of the block B&H is on, killing two and injuring over a dozen. That nearly ended the business, but the B&H community rallied and raised more than $25,000 to help with the rebuild. Then came the pandemic and B&H was once again on the verge of closing. Again, customers from far and wide came to its rescue. "They are our heroes," Ola tells me. "It is the most beautiful thing to me, these people—they become friends and family to us when they walk in here, and you truly understand that bond when things get tough."

People are fanatics when it comes to B&H. That's because of Fawzy, Ola, and their small staff, which includes baker Hugo and beloved counter guy Leo. But the food also helps. This is New York City comfort food at its finest. Stuffed cabbage. Borscht.

Mushroom barley soup. House-baked challah. Cans of Dr. Brown's soda. Blintzes. And then there's one of the craziest things you'll find anywhere: Their iconic whitefish melt consists of chunky house whitefish salad with some yellow American cheese between two slices of buttered challah. It's unlike anything you've ever had. But honestly, I could say that about everything on the menu, even things I've eaten a hundred times before at other places. I ask Ola what the secret is, and she gives me a smile.

"We care. If we didn't care, people wouldn't care about us. So we care. Everything we make we care about."

> **TIP**
>
> **This is a crazy combo, but trust me: Get the mushroom barley soup or borscht and ask them to toss in a matzo ball.**

BALLOON SALOON

133 WEST BROADWAY

I've loved novelty gift shops since I was a kid. You know what I'm talking about: whoopie cushions and those cans that spray streamers of every color of the rainbow. The sort of stuff that makes everybody smile. And I can't think of many places that make you feel like a kid again and realize how badly you need a pair of Groucho Marx glasses quite like Balloon Saloon.

Sharon Hershkowitz and her family have been doing that since 1981. It happened sort of by chance after Sharon and her husband, Jerry, found themselves out of work that same year. They were working in a department store making T-shirts and selling them in a kiosk until the place closed for good. I like that detail about their prior

work experience because it tells you right off the bat that the people who would go on to open Balloon Saloon always wanted to do something fun and creative that made people happy. Out of work and with kids to raise and support, Sharon tried to figure out the next move while keeping an eye out for something along the lines of her last gig.

"It was Jerry's birthday, and I looked in the back of *New York* magazine and saw an ad for a company out on Long Island that sold balloons. So I ordered some. My husband loved that; he was an adventure guy. He said we should go into the balloon business."

So that's what they did. "I had a Volkswagen Rabbit with a little helium tank in the middle. We put an ad in *New York* [magazine] between all these classifieds

for massages and call girls," and the rest is history. They bought a bigger van, put some bullhorns on the hood, had their two kids drive around with them to make drop-offs, and business started to grow. Eventually, they decided it was time to open a shop.

The Balloon Saloon is in a part of Tribeca that used to be known as the shoe district, long before the Odeon and expensive apartment buildings started popping up. "My parents were immigrants," Sharon tells me. They came from Eastern Europe and hardly spoke English, but her father got a job in the shoe business and opened up a shop in the same building where Sharon and her staff now sell bundles of balloons. "There's a legacy here."

TIP

Got a bachelorette party? Balloon Saloon has you covered, from balloons that spell out "Bride" to straws shaped like penises. Like I said, they've got all the necessities.

When you walk in, it's immediate sensory overload in the best possible way. It's like walking into Pee-wee's Playhouse, but everything is for sale. Sharon and her daughter, Tiffany, are almost always around to say hello. Balloon Saloon is also filled with old toys. You'll see robots from the mid-twentieth century, old WWE wrestling dolls, Teenage Mutant Ninja Turtles action figures, life-size replicas of the green Gremlins from the underrated NYC classic *Gremlins 2*. Simply put, it's a great, small family-owned business. It's also nice to know there's a place downtown if you need some fake plastic mustaches, wind-up chattering teeth, or a piñata.

BAZ BAGEL

181 GRAND STREET

Bari Musacchio and her crew make some of the best bagels in Manhattan. And when I say they make them, I mean they hand roll, kettle boil, and bake them right on the premises. Baz feels old school but modern at the same time, and also happens to have one of the best counters for breakfast or lunch in the city.

"The whole idea behind this place was sitting down and eating a bagel," Bari says. "That's it. That was the concept."

Having a concept that simple isn't easy. Baz isn't some hole-in-the-wall, and paying New York City rent and keeping a full staff isn't cheap. And if bagels are the centerpiece of the business, you know they have to be special. That's where Bari's quality control comes in. When I asked her why she decided to go into the bagel business, she told me she had been obsessed with them her entire life. And unlike some Manhattan neighborhoods,

Bari says you gotta get the Baz, a special pumpernickel everything bagel, which comes with scallion cream cheese, lox, tomato, and onion. It's served open-faced, so you can share it. Also get an egg and cheese. It's perfect. Then finish with a black-and-white cookie to go.

TIP

Little Italy was seriously lacking a good bagel spot. "I felt like the neighborhood needed this. It's a place you could bring your grandma or your kid or whoever."

Bari also wanted to make sure she created memories for people while re-creating her own.

"I'd go to the bagel store with my dad and he'd just tell them a dozen of whatever was hot, and I have a very distinct memory of being a kid and leaving the bagel store with the brown paper bag filled with bagels. I remember sitting with it on my lap in the car and that just stuck in my mind." She wants everyone who walks in the door to have that same experience. That's what makes Baz Bagel one of the new NYC institutions. I love it so much that if you watch my 2022 movie *Out of Order*, you might spot it.

CAFFÈ PANNA

77 IRVING PLACE

When you hear that first ice cream truck song playing down the block, it's usually a sign of warmer days ahead. But by around Halloween, the trucks are totally gone. It's like Mister Softee thinks New Yorkers want ice cream only in the summertime. That's not true, but it means you don't really expect to discover some god-tier frozen treats when the weather is cold enough to keep a cone full of sherbet from melting.

When my friend Mike Chau, of the Instagram account @foodbabyny, took me to Caffè Panna for the first time, it was actually snowing out. Some ice cream spots are so good they warrant a trip even during New York's sometimes brutal winters. Mike told me to meet him in front before they opened because there'd be a line. The last part was key. New Yorkers are famously impatient. We walk and talk fast. So when there's something that's attracting a crowd, it's usually worth checking out. Worst-case scenario is it isn't worth the hype, but I don't worry about that when Mike is picking the place.

Caffè Panna was born out of pure obsession. That's how owner Hallie Meyer puts it. "I've always been obsessed with ice cream," she tells me as people line up and

the snow starts to accumulate outside. "I started making it in my parents' kitchen and then I'd sell it in a café on Monday nights," she says. In 2019, she got a storefront up the block from Gramercy Park, the neighborhood where she started making ice cream.

"I started with ten flavors; the idea was I didn't want customers to know what to expect next," and she has kept her word.

If her last name sounds familiar in the context of the food world, it's because Hallie is the daughter of famed restaurateur and Shake Shack founder Danny Meyer. Anyone who has dined at one of her father's establishments knows the guy cares about details and making sure every customer walks out blown away. Saying the apple doesn't fall far from the tree might be underselling his daughter's willingness to take something familiar and totally make customers rethink what they're eating.

"We have six classic flavors you can always depend on," Hallie says. Vanilla, chocolate, a stracciatella that blows minds, the Red Flag strawberry swirl, an Oreo-infused Cookies 'n' Panna, and chocolate sorbet for the vegans; and then the ridiculous Aud's Dream: a sweet and creamy vanilla laced with generous swirls of peanut butter, a gift to her mother who had dreamed of an ice cream exactly like it.

This is incredible ice cream with a side of local anthropology. You wait in line with all the other people, and you hear some good gossip while getting a chance to observe how New Yorkers are when we're standing still.

TIP

Check their Instagram for rotating flavors. Try something new each time you go.

CASA ADELA

66 LOISAIDA AVENUE

You can't have a conversation about New York City culture without talking about the huge contributions of the Puerto Rican community. Just think about one of the most important and ubiquitous parts of the city's landscape, the bodega. After the Spanish-American War ended in 1898, people from the island started making their way to Manhattan. In 1902, local newspaper *The Sun* reported, "New York is to have a bodega. It has struggled along without one for years." The article didn't mention whether or not the owner was from Puerto Rico, but it didn't matter. The bodega came to be known as a little shop that sold everything, and its ties to Caribbean islands including Puerto Rico remain strong: from Jean-Michel Basquiat to Rosie Perez, J.Lo, and Lin-Manuel

TIP

Kick yourself into overdrive with a $2 cup of hot Bustelo.

Miranda to the salsa and reggaeton you'll hear blaring from cars and apartments in the summer. It's even in the way some New Yorkers talk. Go to parts of the city like the Bronx or Washington Heights, and the influence Puerto Rico has had on the modern accent is unmistakable.

You've got to respect the culture in this city, whether it's your own or your neighbor's. That's why I was one of countless New Yorkers in 2021 who got behind Casa Adela when they were facing a rent hike that would have driven them out of business after four decades in the heart of Alphabet City.

"Thankfully, we worked something out, but we'll see," Casa Adela owner, Luis Rivera, tells me one busy afternoon. He's hopeful the deal they made with the landlord will work out. But property owners often overlook how important and beloved certain places are. Casa Adela is a perfect example of that.

My pal Freaky Frige, a born-and-raised Lower East Sider who has been eating at Casa Adela his whole life, points out that a decade or so ago, people were downright afraid of Avenue C. He admits, "There was some bad shit around here." But places like Casa Adela and the community that congregated there offered guidance and helped fuel his creativity. "People really don't understand how deep this community is until they experience it for themselves," says Frige, and Casa Adela is a good place to start toward understanding that.

There's the community—but there's also the food. The rotisserie chicken alone is worth a trip. Add a side of some of the

best rice in the city, some beans, maybe mofongo, a can of Coco Rico, and you've got one of the best meals in Manhattan. It's inexpensive, delicious, and the vibes are unbeatable. Luis wouldn't have it any other way.

"I want everybody to be here," he says. "We serve Puerto Rican food, but it's for anybody. Doesn't matter where you're from."

CASA MAGAZINES

22 EIGHTH AVENUE

I know it's probably tough to believe, given you're reading this in a book filled with great stuff about New York City, but Casa is truly one of the most special places in Manhattan—not just because they have the best selection of magazines and newspapers (around 2,000 titles and fifteen newspapers on sale at any given time), but because of the two guys you'll see there, Mohammed and Ali.

Every place included in this book has some character who makes their neighborhood a little more special. In the case of the Casa guys, whenever I stop in, I feel their love for the community.

Ali tells me Casa Magazines has been around for nearly eighty-five years in one form or another, with Mohammed as its owner since 1994. Ali has been there since the late 1990s. "In my dreams, I worked someplace that was messy, messy, messy," he says as he gestures around at the piles of issues of the *Daily News* next to *The World of Interiors* and a handful of painstakingly created small-press magazines that could sit on your coffee table next to any high-end art books you have out for guests to see.

People talk to each other inside Casa. It's some combination of Mohammed and Ali being great hosts, but there's also all the

TIP

Talk to Ali and Mohammed. Seriously. You should talk to people as much as possible in the city, but these guys know everything and everybody and have lots of amazing stories. Also buy one of their shirts. They've got an incredible merch game.

print everywhere you look. You feel a million miles away from the internet in Casa, and there's something beautiful about that.

Ali thinks it also has to do with the area. This is classic West Village. "It's one of the best places in all of New York City. Everything is old school and the people are so loving and caring."

And it's only a few feet from La Bonbonniere (page 46), another local institution I love. Go hang out with Ali and Mohammed for a bit, grab a copy of *The Paris Review* and some Italian art magazine, walk fifteen seconds to grab some breakfast or lunch, and you've got a perfect start to your day.

CASEY RUBBER STAMPS

322 EAST 11TH STREET

Every now and then you find a place that feels like nowhere else in the city but also totally, 100 percent New York at the same time. Casey Rubber Stamps is one of the best examples of that because it's totally chaotic and cramped whenever I step inside, so it feels pretty normal to a New Yorker. But it's also a shop that makes rubber stamps. I've looked all over, and I don't think there's another place in the city or even in the tri-state area that makes just rubber stamps.

So whenever I show up to visit John Casey at his cramped rubber stamp shop, I'm ready for anything. Once, I went in and remember watching him swearing at a machine. "The piston," he said in his thick Irish accent. "I'm waiting for a damn piston so I can get these people their stamps."

John has been running his shop for more than twenty years, but if he told you he'd been around for fifty or a hundred, you'd believe him. It's everything from John's demeanor as a wise-cracking, foul-

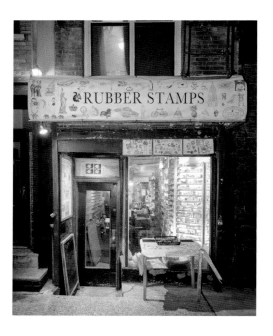

mouthed Irish immigrant, to the eccentric business itself. A personalized rubber stamp is incredibly handy. It looks way cooler than handwriting your address on an envelope or stationery.

John makes the best rubber stamps in the city. He's been doing this his entire life. He got interested in printing as a kid in Ireland and moved to the US with the intention of getting into the business. Today, he's one of the few remaining people in NYC who knows how to do it.

"When I came to New York I was sixteen, and tried to look for equipment. And unfortunately, I was living with nonmechanical spinster aunts, and no family who knew the business," he says with a laugh. It took a few years, but eventually he found a guy on the Lower East Side who sold him his first printer.

As his website says, Casey Rubber Stamps keeps "East Village Artist Hours" and is child-, dog-, and "eccentric-friendly." It's a place for weirdos and creatives. The walls are filled with countless examples of stamps he's made for people over the years. It almost looks like flash tattoo art, with

everything from old occult symbols to the more X-rated stuff. But it all looks classic.

One other thing has always fascinated me about Casey Rubber Stamps.

A few doors down is Veniero's, one of the best pastry shops in Manhattan. So good, it's where my parents bought my first birthday cake. And right next door to Veniero's is Russo's, which has the best mozzarella in the city. So buy some stamps, eat a delicious Italian sandwich, and top it off with a delicious pastry.

TIP

It's a sign on the wall that reads: "Drug Dealers don't use our stamps." John laughs when I mention it, and tells me how back in the 1980s, when dealers all over the neighborhood wanted to literally put their stamp on the product they were selling, John realized he'd become the guy a lot of them went to, and he didn't feel comfortable with it. "I didn't do it deliberately," he says, "but I wish I would have kept some of the ones I made, because a few years ago a museum asked me to reproduce some of them for an exhibition."

Does John consider what he's doing an art or a trade? "It's a craft. It's not *quite* art, not *quite* trade. I do a lot of manipulation of images, but it's still a craft," he says.

CHESS FORUM

219 THOMPSON STREET

Street sports run New York. Go to Brooklyn or the Bronx and catch a game of handball, or go to the Rucker in Washington Heights or the Cage in the West Village to watch street basketball at its finest. But if you want something a little quieter, head to Washington Square Park to catch the chess matches. If you're looking to play, more power to you; but I'd suggest first walking a block over to Chess Forum. For five bucks an hour you can play with anybody who's hanging out, and my friend Imad will talk to you all day about his gathering space for people who love the game that he's made his life's work.

"You can sit here in the summer and there's air-conditioning, in the winter it's warm, the music is always playing, and there's companionship for anybody in the city who wants to just be somewhere," Imad says as violins from the classical music station he keeps on drift out of the speakers. "It's a very noisy city. This is a place for anybody to just come and spend time."

Chess Forum has its roots in the chess parlors once scattered across the city. It was a game anybody could play regardless of the language they spoke or how much or how little money they had. There was once a time when you could find a place to play nearly anywhere in New York City, but now Chess Forum is one of the last holdouts.

Chess Forum is also the place for all your chess set needs. Boards, pieces, and clocks are all for sale. They also offer classes.

TIP

Imad, who came to the United States from Lebanon in 1987, loves to tell stories. One of them is the origin of Chess Forum itself. Imad started playing as a child, and chess helped him get through the horrors of the Lebanese Civil War. There was no electricity, so Imad and some other guys would play the game by candlelight. When he immigrated to the United States, his initial plan was to do a PhD in English at New York University. But one day in 1995, while walking through the Village, he saw a For Rent sign in a Thompson Street window. He told the landlord he didn't have much money, but the building's owner took a chance and said they'd work with him. He got money from friends and family, and he's been around ever since. He's had hard times, especially in 2008 when the economy tanked, iPhones were introduced, and people started getting hooked on their screens. Why play chess IRL when you could just download an app?

But a chess video game is hardly a replacement for the real thing, and chess always has a spot in the culture. These days, Imad says the success of the Netflix series *The Queen's Gambit* has created a whole new generation of players. As he tries to help me get better at my game on a quiet afternoon, he mentions many of the people who have hung out in the space and played chess.

"This was a printing shop before I took over, but before that, it was a chess shop," he tells me. Its patrons included the famous grandmaster Bobby Fischer and Stanley Kubrick among the celebrities who would show up for a game or two. Then Imad mentions two more: "RZA and GZA from Wu-Tang Clan, also." If you didn't think Chess Forum was legit already, the Wu-Tang seal of approval should be all the evidence you need.

COZY SOUP 'N' BURGER

739 BROADWAY

ou can find diners all across the country, but the New York City diner is its own culture. It's the perfect no-frills third space. The menus are a mile long, you get to see some of the best locals you'll find anywhere, and they're peaceful places even when they're packed. Not peaceful as in quiet, since there's always some sort of clanking and rattling going on, but there's something about a place that serves okay coffee and twenty different takes on the omelet that puts people at ease. Call it NYC ASMR.

The diner has long played a part in people's visual understanding of New York City. Edward Hopper was so inspired by a diner near his apartment in the Village that he created *Nighthawks*, one of the most iconic paintings in American history. Martin Scorsese has set scenes in them, Kermit the Frog and his friends hung out in one in *The Muppets Take Manhattan*, and Monk's Café (aka Tom's Restaurant) is the fifth main character on *Seinfeld*. Unfortunately,

as Cozy Soup 'n' Burger owner John Stratidis puts it, "Diners are a dying breed." Sadly, he's not wrong. In 2015, *Crain's New York Business* published an article reporting that about 400 places in the city had either "diner" or "coffee" in their name, and how that was about 1,000 less than a decade or so earlier. This used to be a city filled with simple places where you could sit at a counter or in a booth, read your newspaper, pick at your eggs, and get buzzed on multiple coffee refills, but those kinds of places are getting harder to find.

If the diner is truly a dying breed like John says, Cozy Soup 'n' Burger, the place his family has been running for decades, is one of the last great ones. It *is* cozy, with its two rows of booths up the middle and the counter to the right. The decor is retro cool without trying to be either of those things, and there are a few autographed pictures of some of the establishment's more famous patrons.

I've been eating here since I was a kid, and John or a member of his family has been there every single time. My order: chicken souvlaki "Yanni style" and a cup of split-pea soup. "My dad and uncles came from Greece and opened up the original version under the 59th Street Bridge. It wasn't as big as this one, but it was a blessing that it worked out and they were able to move to this spot in 1982, and we've been here ever since," John says.

John has a degree in mechanical engineering, but he's been working at the diner since he was nine. On Sunday mornings he'd wake up before the sun and beg his dad to take him to work so he could watch and learn. "This place built my foundation and made me who I am today."

Cozy Soup 'n' Burger has helped a lot of other people build their foundations as well. It's a place where generations of NYU students have crammed for tests over plates of French fries and bottomless coffee, including Adam Sandler, who promised John's dad that if he ever became famous, he'd feature the diner in a movie. He made good on his promise by filming Cozy Soup 'n' Burger for 1999's *Big Daddy*. There was one problem. "You must never order the BLT," John says in an accent mimicking Rob Schneider's character, the delivery boy. "Everybody comes in here still gives me shit about the BLT because of Rob Schneider. So when he came in and autographed his photo, he wrote, 'The BEST BLT.'"

Besides having delicious food and being a place where I, countless students, and Adam Sandler all spent time, it's also a pretty good spot if you're looking to find love. John tells the story: "There was once a guy and a girl who came here at the peak part of lunchtime. They didn't know each other, and I told them that unfortunately there was only one booth available, but if they didn't mind sharing it, I could split the check and they could have lunch. They agreed. They sat down, had lunch, and started talking. Guess what? They got married. Only in New York City can you pull something off like that, and that's why this place is so beautiful."

> **TIP**
>
> The split-pea soup is a New York City legend. If you see John, ask him to make you his special creamy, cinnamon-topped "Yanni's Coffee."

MANHATTAN

CULTURE ESPRESSO

307 WEST 38TH STREET

 Midtown has a strange reputation among locals. People seem to go *through* it instead of stay, maybe only for dinner or a Broadway show. But there are a lot of gems in the middle of Manhattan, and many of them go overlooked. One of these, according to my friend Dan Smith, is a coffee shop he tells me is easily one of the best in the entire city. I'm skeptical, but seconds after entering Culture Espresso for the first time, I knew Dan wasn't exaggerating. Everything at Culture, from the baked goods to the art on the merch, but especially the coffee, is there because general manager Johnny Norton likes it.

"I always wanted to open a coffee shop," Johnny says. With over twenty years of experience, he approached the owners of Culture Espresso with a simple idea: an indie coffee shop in the middle of Midtown's sea of chain

TIP

Say what you want about Midtown, but Culture Espresso is worth a stop. It's right between Madison Square Garden and the New York Public Library. Hit the library, grab a coffee and cookie, then see the Knicks play.

restaurants, tourist traps, and Starbucks. All you had to do was serve customers the best stuff. He credits the owners with "taking a chance" and not just opening another basic spot people go in and out of without much thought. "That's a rare thing," he says, "and I think everybody here knows it, so there's a lot of pride in what we do behind the counter. But the people on the other side, the customers, also really care that there's a place like this here."

There's also no place I can think of that makes cookies like Culture Espresso.

"Those are the oatmeal cranberry cookies," Johnny tells me. A woman waiting in line says hello to the GM and then looks at me and says, "Everybody talks about the chocolate chip, but the oatmeal cranberry are the best in the whole city." I didn't want to say I knew that, but Dan had been talking about them for a long time, always telling me I needed to try them.

I finally did. And yeah, I'd walk a few extra blocks for that cookie. It's pretty damn good.

E.ROSSI & COMPANY

193 GRAND STREET

It's always strange to witness people from out of town descend on Lower Manhattan only to go shopping at stores selling things they can get anywhere, from companies that have absolutely zero connection to the city. E.Rossi & Company, on the other hand, has been a Little Italy mainstay since 1910. But the story of the shop that sells everything from little stovetop coffee makers to jerseys and scarves for Italian soccer clubs, local souvenirs, and plenty of wooden spoons for Sunday sauce making, has a story that goes back even further.

"My grandfather, Ernesto Rossi, he came from Naples in 1900 and started out selling newspapers and magazines," Ernie Rossi says. He's the smiling face you see behind the counter of the shop once you've made it past the stacks of toys, T-shirts with Saint Januarius on them, and kitchen items stacked almost to the ceiling. He's one of the last links to turn-of-the-century Little Italy and knows

as much about local history as his own family's.

Ernie's grandfather eventually began selling other products to make money. Coffee pots, pasta-making machines, all sorts of things that were necessities in Italian American households then, and pretty much still are today. "But he was also heavy into music," Ernie says. "He was a music publisher and used to go back to Naples every year. He brought back a lot of singers from Italy to the States. Back then, Mulberry Street was like the Tin Pan Alley of Neapolitan music."

One song connected to neighborhood songwriters is still a Christmastime favorite: "Dominick the Italian Christmas Donkey," recorded by Lou Monte. It's such a part of Italian American tradition that Ernie makes sure to carry shirts and buttons with the blue donkey year-round. "People come in and they go, 'Oh! The donkey! I love the donkey!' They'll buy them in April or May. It doesn't have to be Christmas."

Being able to get Dominick the Italian Christmas Donkey or San Gennaro Feast merch year-round makes E.Rossi & Company the place it is and always has been. It's a Little Italy store first and foremost. It's always going to sell stuff with the neighborhood in mind, and Ernie makes sure his customers— some of whom have been stopping in for decades—know that.

TIP

You are mere feet away from royalty, since Caffé Palermo is a quick turn onto Mulberry when you walk out the door at E.Rossi & Company. Go there not only because you're in Little Italy, where eating a cannoli is mandatory, but because Caffé Palermo's boss, Baby John DeLutro, is literally the Cannoli King. Go there and pay your respects, eat something delicious, and admire the Cannoli King's Hall of Fame, where names like Mel Brooks, Danny DeVito, Jerry Orbach, and other legends are written on the mirror in the back of the restaurant.

ECONOMY CANDY

108 RIVINGTON STREET

conomy Candy started as a pushcart on the Lower East Side before the Great Depression. Back then, the area teemed with European immigrants trying to scrape together a living while living in crowded tenements. "My grandpa grew up in this building we ended up moving into," third-generation owner Mitchell Cohen tells me of his family's connection to the neighborhood. In 1937 the pushcart became a store, and a few years after World War II, Mitchell's grandfather, Morris "Moishe" Cohen, took over the business with his brother-in-law.

"There used to be seven candy stores in the neighborhood," Mitchell says. Economy Candy is a place where you can get sweets from around the globe. Jellybeans, giant rainbow lollipops, and chocolate from all over the world pack its shelves—from Swiss chocolate to Italian nougat, aniseed chews from the UK, Pocky from Japan, and hard-to-find candy bars. Making sure they have anything and everything is a family tradition at Economy. When his grandfather retired, Mitchell's parents took over. When Mitchell grew up, however, he decided to go down a different path: Wall Street. His father ran the family business until Mitchell's wife urged him to step in and keep the tradition going.

The Regal Cinemas down the street is pretty great because they have reclining chairs and don't really check for outside food. So stock up on candy and eat it while you watch a movie.

TIP

Today, Economy Candy is an institution. They don't advertise, but word of mouth takes care of that. Besides location, selection, and history, one more thing makes people remember Economy Candy: its logo. It depicts a happy little kid with a head of hair that turns into a swirling curl, his arms spread and wearing a red T-shirt with his belly peeking out. It looks part Japanese anime, part Winnie the Pooh. Turns out the logo is a caricature of Mitchell. He's not just the third-generation owner, but the literal face of one of the most famous logos in the entire city.

FISHS EDDY

889 BROADWAY

A place doesn't need a plaque to be considered a landmark. To me, the Empire State Building or the Brooklyn Bridge are as important as Lexington Candy or Punjabi Deli. Fishs Eddy also ranks among the most special places in the city not recognized by the National Register of Historic Places. It's not somewhere people go to sit and eat, or have a conversation over a cup of coffee. And *technically* it's not a landmark, but I think all the people who have gone there to buy dishes, mugs, and plates since 1986 might disagree.

"I know it's important to people, and that's important to me," owner Julie Gaines says. Julie is as much a legend as her store is. Everybody knows her. She's one of the nicest and funniest people you'll meet around Union Square. What started out as a crazy idea to buy a barnful of old American dishware has become an obsession and legacy. "When this is gone, there isn't anybody else doing it," Julie adds.

That's because as colorful and lively as the vast (by Manhattan standards) store is,

Fishs Eddy serves as a link to an industry that no longer exists in the US. Forget the countless roadside diners and little coffee shops scattered across the country that have given way to Starbucks; America's restaurant-ware industry is gone. Look under any mug, and it will likely say it was made in China. Julie's mission has been to collect the last reminders of a once-thriving industry. She's tirelessly searched for the last lots of high-quality glassware and dishes like the sort our grandparents once used.

But Fishs Eddy isn't a vintage shop. The store is also filled with new drinking glasses covered in all sorts of art, from art deco design to the famed "Heroes of the Torah" depicting famous rabbis. They sell coffee cups with pigeons politely telling you to "fuck off" and tea towels with midcentury cowboy prints. New York City quirk is an actual thing, and Fishs Eddy is the embodiment of it. It's been around for a long time, but you discover something dope every time you go in. It's a fun institution people go to when they want an entire dinnerware set or just a new thing to drink coffee from. They sell stuff everybody needs, but the dishes and cups at Fishs Eddy are always going to be cooler than anything you could find at a chain store or Ikea.

TIP

Ask Julie about her plate and mug museum upstairs. She loves to give tours. It's one of the coolest collections of old dishes, saucers, cups, and other old diner relics. Also, Julie's son, Ben Lenovitz, is an artist and has a gallery in the back where he will paint your pet's portrait. I have commissioned two for my dog, Toby.

MANHATTAN

GRANDMA'S PLACE

84 WEST 120TH STREET

here are a lot of good people in New York City, and then there's Grandma Dawn Martine. She's a saint.

"This whole building was abandoned. And in 1999, when they started renovating it, I realized I was going to have a laundromat or fish and chips joint next door to where I live. Since I was a schoolteacher at the time, and many of my students' parents didn't read, I decided to open a literacy center here," she tells me.

She operated the center for five years. "I taught seventy-year-olds how to read

the Bible, and I also taught seven-year-olds."

Then, of course, the landlord did what landlords do and doubled the rent. Grandma Dawn couldn't afford it, but she had 25,000 books next door, so she put them in the literacy center and started selling them. That helped ease the burden a little, so Grandma Dawn added some toys and games to sell. "And that's how it became a store."

The place became vital to the community, but the landlord kept raising the rent more and more. The current

But it's about the kids first and foremost. Grandma Dawn always encourages the children who live in the neighborhood to do well in school and also helps instill a good work ethic in them. Local kids who bring her report cards showing good grades or who help with chores around the shop can walk out of Grandma's Place with a toy or book of their choosing. Not a bad deal.

Hopefully, Grandma's Place sticks around for decades to come and nurtures the minds and imaginations of new generations of local kids. But in the meantime, Grandma Dawn has her sights set elsewhere. She isn't leaving, but she's been working to establish a mobile Grandma's Place, a bookmobile that drives around Harlem and provides free books to kids all over the neighborhood.

"I have a nonprofit for the bookmobile now, but my accountant, he said, 'Grandma, usually when a business doesn't make any money in five or six years, the IRS thinks it's a hobby or a tax dodge and they take them off the map. I've been doing this for over twenty years, and they let me continue. I've never made a cent."

Like I said, she's a saint.

amount, "they tell me, is a bargain," she says. And maybe it is . . . for a Starbucks. Watching somebody like Grandma Dawn go through such headaches and heartaches is especially crushing. Her small book and toy shop *is* a business, but it's also a service. Anytime I go there, a dozen kids stream through, picking up children's books about Martin Luther King Jr., *Brilliant Baby Fights Germs*, educational games, puppets, everything. Grandma Dawn serves her community by offering a place that has helped people of all ages grow and learn since back when it wasn't considered a desirable neighborhood the way it is now.

TIP

You can have a perfect day walking up through Central Park to Grandma's Place, ten blocks up from the northern edge of the park. While you're in the neighborhood you can stop for chicken and waffles at Amy Ruth's, visit the Graffiti Hall of Fame, and see the Museum of the City of New York.

GREENWICH LOCKSMITHS

56 SEVENTH AVENUE SOUTH

If there's one truth that resonates throughout all five boroughs, it's that New York City is a place filled with so many wonders that it's easy to miss one or a hundred whenever you walk out the door. It could be a gargoyle on the roof of an old brick building you've passed a thousand times and never noticed, or a statue obscured by trees and brush in one of the city's many parks. There are always things to miss, which means there are endless chances for discovery. Few places sum up that idea as well as the odd 125-square-foot structure along Seventh Avenue South that countless people walk or bike past every single day.

In theory, Greenwich Locksmiths shouldn't be hard to miss. Anyone who has spent some time walking around the Village has likely seen the unique little shop with thousands of keys painstakingly attached to its facade. If they take a closer look, they'll realize that shop owner Phil Mortillaro has used the space as a canvas to re-create Van Gogh's *Starry Night*.

TIP

Phil can turn your everyday house key into a beautiful custom object. He has many styles ranging from ornate European skeleton keys to vintage NYC subway token keys.

Even though technology changes so much else, locksmiths are always necessary, especially in New York City. Phil opened up in 1980. Back then, the neighborhood was hardly as expensive or trendy as it is today. He probably could have found something bigger, but it didn't matter. He realized right away, "It's perfect." Now in his seventies, Phil feels the same love for his shop and his work as he did back then. "You gotta understand, there are a lot of other businesses that are forty or forty-five years old, but not with the original owners. I'm the original guy that actually started this one." He's still busy making keys all the time, but his son, Phil Jr., has been working by his side for years and looks to keep the family business going for years to come.

Phil is a philosophical guy. That's part of the reason some people will take a bus or train, even if it's out of their way, to have Phil make their key. Getting a key made is one of those mundane experiences we all have to deal with, like getting a prescription filled or going to the post office to mail a package. Phil figured out how to make what he does fun and interesting. He's always up for a conversation and has a million stories. But when you find yourself talking with him, something might dawn on you: This guy is a locksmith in a city filled with millionaires and billionaires. He makes keys that don't cost more than a few bucks. He's not exactly making Elon or Bezos money here. And that's where the beauty lies in what Phil and countless others all across the city do. They don't do their jobs because they're going to get rich—it's because they care. Phil loves what he does, and it shows.

"You don't need a lot. Once you get away from the keeping up with the Joneses bullshit, you're okay," he says. "Do what you wanna do."

THE HOT DOG KING

FIFTH AVENUE & EAST 82ND STREET, IN FRONT OF
THE METROPOLITAN MUSEUM OF ART

Mel Brooks famously said, "It's good to be the king." Dan Rossi won't argue with that, but he might add that it takes a hell of a lot of work to keep the crown of New York's hot dog king, including sleeping in his van, arguing with police and politicians, and fighting for other vendors trying to make a living from food carts.

"But that's the way things go," Rossi says as he squirts mustard on a dog.

It's an unfortunate truth, and partly why the hot dog vendor is a dying breed. This city used to be filled with carts that sold good hot dogs, along with pretzels, knishes, and all sorts of other things you could munch on between meals. While vendors still abound, their quality has gone downhill. That's not something you want to hear when it comes to street meat. But there's a reason that more than a century ago a guy like Nathan Handwerker could start selling nickel dogs on Coney Island and turn it into the empire that is Nathan's Famous. They're hot dogs, sure. But they're part of the New York story, and the people who serve them have to deal with more bullshit now than ever before.

Dan is the quintessential little guy in NYC. And I don't mean that in a demeaning way. He's a tough blue-collar Bronx native who served in Vietnam, came back home, and wanted to be his own boss. His body hurts, he's got to deal with plenty of bureaucracy-induced headaches, but Dan and his daughter, Elizabeth—also a veteran—wouldn't want to do anything else.

New Yorkers have been buying food from pushcarts, stands, and trucks for generations. Today around 20,000 street vendors work across the city. Some of them have eked out a decent living, but ask any person on the corner serving buttered rolls and coffee or pretzels and knishes, they'll all have similar experiences to share. One day the cops want to ticket you or the health department wants to shut you down. The next day drunk customers act like bozos, your generator stops working, or the weather rains out most of your sales for the day. As for Dan, the reason the king sleeps in his van isn't because he doesn't have a palace to live in—he doesn't want to lose his prime spot.

"He knows this business inside and out," Elizabeth tells me as a line forms outside her dad's cart. "He's been at this location in front of the Metropolitan Museum of Art since July 2007 and he's seen everything." She looks at him and smiles. She's proud of her dad and the work they do. She says it's great to work alongside him, with the only problem being "We're too similar."

I don't know the ins and outs of the Rossi family, but from where I stand, that doesn't seem like such a bad thing. Dan and Elizabeth work hard to make sure people get the best hot dog they can find, selling about 300 on a good day. So in case you were wondering, that's the number of franks it takes to become New York royalty.

TIP

Elizabeth says the true New York cart dog is served with spicy brown mustard and sauerkraut and, if you want, some of the Hot Dog King's famous red-onion sauce.

MANHATTAN

43

KATZ'S DELICATESSEN

205 EAST HOUSTON STREET

atz's has been around since 1888. It has earned its icon status and then some. It's become a tourist attraction, but real New Yorkers will tell you it's an important part of the city, like Grand Central or Yankee Stadium. It's impossible to imagine the city without it. That's why it ended up in this book. It's pretty easy to put it on a list of the best spots in New York because it's so famous. But the thing is that it deserves all the praise and more.

Third-generation owner Jake Dell wasn't sure he was going to get into the family business as a kid. "I thought I was going to be a doctor. But I probably knew after a year of working here that I was here for life," he says. "That first holiday rush was probably the first time I realized that. There's just something magical about December in New York City. It really comes alive, and this place has that same energy. All of that chaos, it was great. I couldn't shake it."

the corned beef, the Reuben, the latkes, the matzo ball soup, the hot dogs, and everything else they serve. "I don't try to push anything on anybody," Jake says. "I let people know a deli is more than a pastrami sandwich. There's a lot going on here. The traditional Jewish-style delicatessen is not one meal or one sandwich: It's about the meat."

And it's also, Jake says, about the lines to get the meat. "Understand how each cutter has their own line. A lot of tourists get that wrong, but you see New Yorkers weaving, going to a line." And New Yorkers, Jake says, know how to talk to the guys cutting the meat. "You interact with the cutter. You specify how you want it. Tell them you want it fatty, less fatty. Talk to them. Have that conversation."

Order a hot dog and eat it while waiting in line for a pastrami sandwich. You won't need to eat for the rest of the day.

TIP

That energy extends beyond the twelfth month of the year. "I come here every day and see glee. Just pure glee."

People love Katz's. It's sort of impossible not to. While famous for having some of the best pastrami, its connection to Billy Crystal and Meg Ryan's famous scene in *When Harry Met Sally* is just as well-known as its cured meat. But Katz's is way more than just pastrami and Sally's fake orgasm; salami is a big part of the deli's story, as is

MANHATTAN

45

LA BONBONNIERE

28 EIGHTH AVENUE

ew Yorkers take breakfast seriously. Egg and cheese. Bagel with butter. Cup of coffee. These are sacred rituals. But brunch is a whole other thing. I find that most brunch spots are overrated, overpriced, and overcrowded. One of my only exceptions is La Bonbonniere, one of the last truly great greasy spoons in New York specializing in brunch.

"The French toast is the favorite, but I love an omelet with feta, tomato, and onions," says co-owner Marina Cortez Arrieta. Like so many people in the city, Marina is an immigrant. She came from Peru more than thirty years ago and realized her American dream while working at the best little diner in the West Village. She busted her ass and became a business partner with owner Gus Maroulletis. The place had been

"He'd always drink a glass of milk and have a grilled cheese." She even recalls what he ate the last time he came in before passing away in 2013: "Egg salad sandwich."

But don't let the big names fool you. There's no velvet rope to get into La Bonbonniere. It's not a celeb hot spot and not expensive. What it is is a true New York spot. Somewhere to go and drink some coffee as you read the newspaper or magazine you just got a few doors down at Casa Magazines (page 22), or have breakfast with an old friend. You can listen to other people gossip or zone out to the sound of dishes clanking and the spatula hitting the stovetop. It's the best place to start your day or take a break in the middle of it.

La Bonbonniere is one of two food spots in the city where they've named a sandwich after me. If you're in the mood, try the New York Nico turkey club. It's the best in town. Also, just a heads-up: They don't take credit cards so come with cash.

around for longer than either of them (some estimates range anywhere from eighty-five to ninety-five years), but it's because of Marina and Gus that the place has stayed a local landmark with a lot of famous New Yorkers among its regulars. "Philip Seymour Hoffman was a regular," Marina says. "A beautiful man. I miss him." Then she points to another picture of a favorite customer of hers who is no longer around, James Gandolfini.

LA SIRENA MEXICAN FOLK ART

27 EAST 3RD STREET

ew York City is obviously my heart and soul, but I understand that it's important to get out sometimes. For Dina Leor, owner and proprietor of La Sirena, her escape was to Mexico. "The first time I went, I felt like I was home," she says.

But since she actually lives and works in NYC, she figured out a way to make it feel as though she were in Mexico. On her first trip to Mexico, when she was nine years old, she visited Puerto Vallarta, "back when it was more of a fishing village," and not the

huge tourist destination it is today. "I'd go there and lay on the ground or climb trees, and just watch people and hang out." Her love for Mexico has become a lifelong obsession, but she never imagined opening a store spotlighting Mexican art. "I'm an art therapist, working at Bellevue, and the only thing that would recharge me was going to Mexico. I'd buy stuff but I didn't realize I was obsessed with folk art until my home and classroom kept filling up. So I started having little sales for the teachers, then I started selling on St. Marks

TIP

This is where I get many of my Christmas ornaments. Everything you get at La Sirena is pretty tough to find outside of Mexico, and they really make your tree stand out.

and downs, but there's something special about her store that keeps people coming back. Part of it is quirk, the fact that there isn't anything else like it nearby, and the neighborhood it's in was always known for that. Places like La Sirena, niche specialty stores owned by eccentrics and artists, used to be easier to find in and around St. Marks, but they've been pushed out by high rent and the big corporate businesses that can afford it. Because of that, a lot of the charm has been stripped away. That alone would be enough reason to visit La Sirena. But the truth is, I can't go there and not walk out with something. And when Dina and I chat for a few minutes, I notice that every single customer who walks in has the same great problem.

Place." In November 1999, she finally opened her shop.

All these years later, the little store is crammed full of trinkets and art from all over Mexico. Pottery, Baja hoodies, handmade huaraches, all sorts of one-of-a-kind jewelry, lucha libre masks, you name it.

Like any small-business owner—and La Sirena is truly small—Dina has had her ups

LEE LEE'S BAKED GOODS

283 WEST 118TH STREET

Rugelach is one of those confections so good I expect to find it everywhere I go outside of NYC, yet that's not always the case. It's not a native New York baked good like the bagel or pastrami; it's one of those treats that either came over with or was popularized by Eastern European Jewish immigrants in the early twentieth century, and ended up a city staple. You can get good rugelach almost anywhere in the city, but if you want the top-tier stuff, go to Harlem and see Alvin Lee Smalls, aka Mr. Lee.

"I started baking sixty years ago," he tells me as I spot a tray of fresh rugelach coming out of the oven. Mr. Lee explains how he came to New York from South Carolina as a young man in the early 1960s and worked in the kitchen at New York-Presbyterian Hospital. "I was peeling a lot of onions," he says with a smile.

I imagine going home smelling like onions isn't the best thing on a hot summer night. That's probably why Mr. Lee walked into the hospital bakery one day and

TIP

Rugelach makes a great gift. And it travels well. I recommend the gift tin, which contains 26 pieces.

thought, "Let me try my hand at this." He wasn't a baker, but he was eager to learn. And in the hospital bakery he learned how to bake classic staples like Danish and pies.

Mr. Lee became obsessed with rugelach. He wanted to make it better than anyone else but also a little differently. So he started baking rugelach that dwarfed most others in size while trading the traditional hard, crumbly, and cookie-like texture for something with a little give.

He opened his first bakery in 1988 but it closed after six years. His second shot came in 2001. He opened a new shop, and things took off from there. Once people discovered Mr. Lee's rugelach, it didn't matter if they were from up the street, from the Bronx, Brooklyn, or anywhere else in the city, they started showing up. His rugelach got so famous that Mr. Lee's birthday, April 29, became enshrined as National Rugelach Day in 2022.

Mr. Lee is proud of his association with rugelach along with everything else he's made, as well as his place in the community. Mr. Lee *is* Mr. Rugelach, but as he'll be the first to tell you, everything he makes is good—the black-and-white cookie, for instance. I've had my share of this iconic New York treat, but I have a hard time thinking of many places that make it better than he does. The coffee cake is also ridiculous, and the way he makes a Danish will make you forget about all the other ones you've ever had.

LEXINGTON CANDY SHOP

1226 LEXINGTON AVENUE

Believe it or not, Lexington Candy Shop, a place that makes one of the best egg creams in the Western world, is where you go to detox. People don't go there to type on their laptops or look at their phones; you have a chat with the guys behind the counter, read your newspaper, and try to get back in touch with the real world that's not online. Owner John Philis has made it his mission to keep it that way.

John's grandpa opened the place in 1925. Back then, it actually was a candy store. Five years later, in 1930, John's dad came over from Greece and started working in the burgeoning family business. The place

has been passed down from one Philis to the next ever since. Besides that, not much has changed.

"We haven't changed much in about seventy-five years. The way you see it today is the way you'd see it in 1948," John tells me

as the server brings over my plate of French toast. "People from all over the world come here to just sit at the counter and eat. It's a counter, not a bar. We make a big thing about that. We're behind the counter and the people on the other side talk sports, finance, world affairs. I've watched a lot of friendships spring up over time because of that."

Over the years, many New Yorkers and out-of-towners have come through these doors. It just has that iconic look to it, the sort of place that people who have never been here imagine is commonplace in the city but is sadly one of very few left.

But even more important than the way the place looks is the consistency and quality of what they serve. "If it ain't broke, don't fix it" is really the way Lexington Candy Shop works. But an addition to that motto could be, "But if it is broke, have a backup." John points to the beautiful milkshake machine that looks like it's made of Jadeite glass. It's one of those classic art deco beauties they stopped making fifty years ago. He calls it the Green Machine and repeats it to make sure I know its name. "We have a new one downstairs. The new one is twenty or thirty years old, so not *really* new. But I used to have to bring it up when the Green Machine had to go to the shop and people would get really upset. They'd bother me, ask me when it's coming

back, if I'm sure it's coming back, so I needed a backup. I found another Green Machine so I don't have to listen to people complain."

Just to be safe, there's now a third Green Machine. "A girl came in right after I got the second one. She said she had one because her boyfriend wanted it, but they broke up and she didn't want it around anymore. All it needed was a new cord, and I could take care of that. So I made her an offer, and now that's one less thing to worry about."

One thing he isn't worried about is the stream of customers who come in asking for a Coke float. People are obsessed with the shop's famous mix of Coke syrup, soda water, and ice cream. When I posted a video of it on Instagram, it went crazy viral. Go there and it's pretty likely you'll see somebody drinking one.

> **TIP**
> You can't come here without getting the Coke float. Make sure they serve it in an old-fashioned Coca-Cola glass for the best experience.

MAMA'S TOO!

2750 BROADWAY

I think the Upper West Side is actually underrated as a great pizza neighborhood. I say that simply because of Frank Tuttolomondo's singular mission to create the perfect slice of pizza. He never gets too crazy with his pies and serves traditional triangle slices, but what Mama's Too! specializes in is

square slices. Does he call them "Grandma slices" or "Sicilian"?

"Neither," he says. "The conception of this place was to not adhere to any style. We wanted something different, so we called it Mama's Too! style because nobody is doing what we do."

He's not exaggerating. You've never seen pizza like Frank's. The color and flavor of the house pie, with a couple of pieces of basil on top of the melted cheese and red sauce, is incredible. The pepperoni forms into cups of the spicy Italian salami, not the flat little discs—cups. They're very particular about that. Then start working your way through specialty pies you won't find anywhere else: Try the 18th Avenue with fennel sausage, house-roasted peppers, and whipped ricotta; and next maybe go for the slice with poached pears, sweet gorgonzola, aged mozz, and hot honey.

Frank says, "Around the block, we have Mama's Pizza. That's where I started. That's where my grandma and my mom's side started in the business. My grandma turned ninety-five and wanted to retire, and she asked me if I wanted to take over. I said yes, then dropped out of college and started in the business." He learned the ropes and then took it from there, running the business until he believed he learned enough to try something different.

One day a week, they do sandwiches that are the stuff of local legend. People make a hobby of finding out what Frank will be selling from week to week, and he's done everything from a chicken parm that will put you in a wonderful food coma to a porchetta au jus with broccoli rabe and some provolone. He posts what he's making on Instagram.

"My family has been doing this a long time," he says. "I take this seriously, and that's why people are out there waiting to order it every day. I appreciate seeing that."

MERCER STREET BOOKS

206 MERCER STREET

It's sad to say, but Mercer Street Books feels like the last of a dying breed. It's not that there aren't great places that still sell used books in Manhattan, but the little shop in the middle of NYU's campus stands out because of its selection. That's because founder and owner Wayne Conti is an obsessive reader, so he tries to apply quality control as much as possible. You can go to Mercer Street and find a secondhand copy of *Moby-Dick* or a dog-eared *Just Kids* by Patti Smith that somebody didn't have space for on their bookshelf anymore, and you'll also find first editions, old pulp novels, rare photography books, and vintage paperbacks. But Wayne didn't just show up one day in 1990 and decide to open a bookstore at 206 Mercer.

"I was a customer here," he says. "This would be from 1984 to 1990. It was called The Art of Reading. Before that, in the 1960s, it was a libertarian bookstore. And before that—and this explains the lighting—it was a Chicken Delight."

Wayne moved to New York to be a writer. And like countless poets and

novelists before and since, he turned to bookselling to pay the bills. Walk into the Strand, Greenlight, or Books Are Magic, and it's likely at least one employee there is working on a manuscript. Wayne had some success as a writer, but the money wasn't really coming in. He worked a bunch of odd jobs to pay the bills, and eventually saw an opportunity to take over the space when problems arose between the previous bookstore tenants and the landlord. "The landlord was reasonable, so we worked out an idea and opened this."

Those kinds of stories used to be common in New York. You could agree on a number, get the money together, and open up shop. It's not that easy anymore. Wayne saw how difficult that was leading up to 2020 when construction on the block wiped out foot traffic. Then, when COVID-19 shut the city down, almost all bookstores were

They have a great selection of old photography books. Also a lot of great books about New York City.

TIP

left to wonder if and when they would see customers again. Thankfully, Mercer Street Books has a lot of fans. Authors like Zadie Smith and Jeremiah Moss lent their voices to the chorus of people who raised more than $60,000 to help Wayne stay open. I found out just how much people love the place after I posted something about the troubles the shop faced. A few days later, there was a line out the door because New Yorkers love to read and don't want to lose a bookstore that's become an institution.

"People love used books. The books come out, and then sometimes they go out of print eventually. So if you're a reader, this little bookstore might provide more interesting titles than a Barnes & Noble, but it also feels like you're getting something that's one of a kind. Each one is unique," Wayne says.

MANHATTAN

57

MR. THROWBACK

437 EAST 9TH STREET

'm sure this will come as no shock to you, but the person with one of the most well-curated collections of vintage sports merch around isn't actually named Mr. Throwback on his birth certificate. But that doesn't stop people from greeting him by the name of his shop when he's walking around the neighborhood. That's because if you want something from the 1990s and early 2000s, he's your guy. As for older stuff, you'll find

plenty of 1970s and 80s mixed in, depending on when you stop by. But how did he get the name?

"I didn't want to just be something like 'Jim's Vintage Store.' I went with Mr. Throwback because 'Mr.' is a sign of respect, and I wanted to be respected in this game. When you think Mr. Throwback, you know where you're getting it," he tells me.

The best vintage places are run by obsessives. Mr. Throwback digs through mountains of T-shirts to find one perfect 1994 New York Rangers Stanley Cup championship shirt. When I stop by, a customer pulls a John Starks jersey off the rack and Mr. Throwback educates them on what year the jersey came out just by looking at the tag. "The felt patch tells you it's pre-1995," he says.

Mr. Throwback was inspired to go into business by an old yellow-and-green Shawn Kemp Seattle Supersonics jersey he found in his dresser. "I put it on and was amazed it still fit, and I just got really obsessed with collecting them. At some point, I realized I had over two hundred, so I started selling them on eBay." From there, Mr. Throwback's obsession with 1990s sports turned into a brick-and-mortar business. Today, he's got everything from the NBA, NHL, MLB, NFL,

college sports, the Olympics, whatever. You name it and he's probably got it.

"But this is by far our most popular seller," Mr. Throwback says as he pulls out a shirt depicting Jennifer Aniston, as Rachel from *Friends*, wearing a Knicks sweatshirt from the 1990s. The shirt has become a local staple, something people sitting courtside at the Garden wear. "Ten years straight, people keep buying it. The guy who wrote *Friends* wore it on the reunion episode. His son shops here all the time and he's a big Lakers fan, but he knows that even in New York, if he comes to Mr. Throwback, he's going to find the best stuff from his team."

TIP

Right across the street is Throwback 2, which Mike opened in 2024 and specializes in non-sports-related throwback goods. You can't visit one without checking out the other.

MUSIC INN WORLD INSTRUMENTS

169 WEST 4TH STREET

usic Inn World Instruments represents old, weird Greenwich Village. It's been in the same location more than sixty years. Whenever I walk in, there's some sort of jam session going on. Sometimes it's jazz, sometimes it's a guy fingerpicking a banjo. Chances are if you hang out long enough, somebody will play a song from the neighborhood's days as the epicenter of the American folk scene, from Lead Belly and Woody Guthrie to Bob Dylan.

"The guy who started this store in 1958 was a Korean War vet," owner Jaff Slatnick tells me. "He married a girl who had some money, and they went in on this store. I came in late 1967, just before Christmas." Jeff looks and sounds like a wizard, with his bushy white beard and big circular glasses that give him an owl-eye stare. He was playing a gig nearby at the Electric Circus, the famed St. Marks Place venue that hosted the likes of the Grateful Dead and Velvet Underground. "I could play the sitar, and the owner told me he was looking for somebody who could help sell those."

In the late 1960s, thanks to Ravi Shankar's influence on the Beatles and the Rolling Stones, people wanted to learn the Indian instrument. So Jeff started selling

TIP

Music Inn hosts a great open mic every Thursday that gets everybody from jam band musicians to rappers to stand-up comics.

to full-time when the original owner stopped coming in and eventually willed the store to Jeff. I can't say what it was like forty or fifty years ago, but I'm going to guess it hasn't changed much since then.

Jeff's life is interesting enough, but so are the instruments in his shop. Like the oldest one he has: It literally looks like it was made from a fallen tree in the forest.

"The oldest instrument here is from Japan. It's called a wagon. They don't make them anymore; they made them about a thousand years ago and they evolved into the koto. This is one that's still alive. It's just a tree branch," he says. When and where he got it, he's not sure. With so many memories surrounding him, it seems fine if he doesn't recall one or two.

sitars at the shop during the Christmas season. Then he returned to California, where he'd been gigging around. In 1976, he found his way back East. He played sitar at a Midtown Indian restaurant while working part-time at the Music Inn. Part-time turned

MANHATTAN

MYZEL'S CHOCOLATES

140 WEST 55TH STREET #1

eed a candy fix? You can go into any bodega and just grab a Snickers bar or bag of Skittles for a buck or two . . . or you can visit Kamila at Myzel's Chocolates. She's been selecting the sweets she lovingly stocks in her shop since 1990. She's got stuff you won't find anywhere else, including the best versions of some favorites, such as chocolate-covered pretzels, chocolate-dipped strawberries, and chocolate truffles.

All that chocolate, and it's not even the first thing many people think of when they walk into Myzel's. Kamila is the queen of licorice. Although chocolate is part of the shop's name, its main draw is licorice—more than 150 kinds from all over the world, all in jars lining the shop walls.

Kamila came to New York in the early 1980s as a political refugee from Poland. She spent a few years getting to know her new country the way countless people from all over the globe do. Some stay, others go. Kamila loved New York, so staying wasn't a

TIP

Kamila takes pride in decorating the shop for every holiday—Christmas, Thanksgiving, Valentine's Day, Easter, etc. Make sure to stop by and ask her about any holiday specials.

tough call. Eventually, though, she wanted to do something on her own, something that brought her happiness. That's the American Dream, right? Do your own thing and be happy. And candy is one of the things almost all of us can agree makes people happy.

While Kamila has countless dedicated customers, she also has had to deal with the ups and downs of owning a small business. One of the hardest times came during the COVID-19 pandemic, when Myzel's nearly closed because of all the business they lost when Broadway shut down and foot traffic vanished. But Kamila and her shop are so beloved, a GoFundMe netted over $100,000 to keep the sweets shop open.

When things started getting back to normal, I went there and noticed something that was tough to see during the pandemic. It made me understand why, besides the friendly owner and the delicious candy she sells, Myzel's is the sort of place locals would want to keep around. It's because Midtown is a part of the city that's always in motion, and it's really easy *not* to stop at Myzel's. But those who know about it make sure they pop in because there's something so old school about what Kamila does. It's a nice break from everything else going on outside.

ORO LATINO JEWELRY

82 BOWERY

ew York City has its share of legendary jewelers who sell chains to rappers and pinkie rings to wise guys. But I go to Tommy Jewels, owner of Oro Latino Jewelry, for anything that shines.

"This is a family business. We've been around over thirty years," he tells me as I scope the gold pendants: a pot leaf, a Yankees logo, a Star of David, some crosses, slices of pizza, and basically anything else you can think of. "We deal mostly with local media, but social media blew us up."

He's underselling it. Tommy's family is famous for making golden rope necklaces and Jesus pieces for NYC rappers, from big names to a thousand other guys you've never heard of. They go to Tommy because he's got old-school influences. "All the diamond stuff, those sort of crazy pieces, I love those. But I'm a gold guy. I grew up in the nineties. Watching *Video Music Box* after school hit when I was a kid; I wanted to be like those guys."

> **TIP**
> Tommy does custom stuff with a quick turnaround. If he does something for you, then you can flex on your friends that you have a one-off from Tommy Jewels.

Back in the day, "those guys" were members of Wu-Tang Clan, including Raekwon, who came in before his iconic 1995 solo album *Only Built 4 Cuban Linx . . .* dropped. "They came in and took pictures, but I don't think he knew how well the album would do, because he was going solo. Later that same month he came back and said, 'Okay, I'm ready now.' He ordered a chain with a dragon pendant on it, the same one you see him wearing on the album cover." But there was one problem. "He came back and was like 'The album is called *Cuban Linx* and I'm not wearing a Cuban link.' He had the piece on a figaro chain. So we swapped out the chain for a Cuban link."

Now rappers and everybody else who loves gold show up to Canal Street rather than the Diamond District. Tommy's the man you want to talk to. He'll take care of you.

PAGEANT PRINT SHOP

69 EAST 4TH STREET

Sooner or later it happens to all of us. The cheap reproduction posters we hang on our walls with thumb tacks or tape stop cutting it. You want something classier, possibly rare, or even one of a kind. That's where sisters Shirley and Rebecca Solomon at Pageant Print Shop come in.

"Mostly I'm looking for New York material," Shirley says. "People come in all the time trying to sell stuff. They're cleaning up, moving, things like that. We've got a warehouse filled with more prints."

The shop itself isn't that huge, but you could easily spend a few hours browsing. It's almost like a museum, except you can buy just about everything from antique maps of the Lower East Side from the early 1900s to vintage *New Yorker* covers to vintage illustrations of beef cuts that would look great framed in your kitchen. There's plenty to look at, as well as a special connection to old New York City.

"My father, Sidney B. Solomon, and his partner, Henry "Chip" Chafetz, opened Pageant in 1946 as a used book shop," Shirley says.

Pageant was originally located on Fourth Avenue, not Fourth Street, and Fourth Avenue was known as Book Row

Random Accessories NYC is down the block. It's a great spot for gifts and tchotchkes.

TIP

since the late nineteenth century and well into the 1960s. At its height, nearly fifty bookstores were located up and down the avenue. That's part of the reason for New York's reputation as a literary city. Yeah, the big publishing houses are here, but having so many places to purchase reasonably priced books also helped. Shirley and Rebecca's father and his business partner eventually moved into other areas adjacent to the rare book trade, including reprinting important out-of-print books like Henry Roth's *Call It Sleep* and selling rare prints and maps.

In 2005, the sisters made the move to the current location, and it's been a neighborhood staple ever since. And even though there's so much to look through, Shirley doesn't hesitate when I ask what sells the most.

"Maps of the East Village."

PEARL RIVER MART

452 BROADWAY

I don't understand why people come to New York to shop at stores also found where they live. Whether it's the shirts and bootleg stuff on Canal Street or the niche shops that focus on cookbooks or international spices, the mom-and-pop stores have more personality, stories, and, frankly, better stuff. Nowhere is this represented better than at Pearl River Mart.

If you know anyone who moved to New York to go to college, you've likely heard of it. Going to Pearl River Mart is a rite of passage providing everything from Japanese snacks to Mandarin dresses. The one thing they probably wouldn't sell you is what you'll see the store's eightysomething founder, Mr. Chen, walking around in. If you see an older guy in a denim Pearl River vest, say hi. He's a legend. When I ask Pearl River Mart president Joanne Kwong if I can buy one, she tells me, "That's for employees only. Mr. Chen shows up to work five days a week dressed to drive our truck."

Still?

"We got him to take a day off, but Mr. and Mrs. Chen love being here," Joanne says.

I get why. Pearl River Mart is like no place else. Open since 1971, Pearl River was one of the only places you could get authentic Chinese goods back when diplomatic relations between the United States and China were frozen. Mr. Chen moved heaven and earth to bring inventory from his homeland to New York's Chinatown so people could feel more comfortable in their new country. "We're the first Chinese American department store," Joanne tells me. "Mr. Chen used to smuggle stuff illegally, so we know we're the first."

Today, Pearl River Mart carries products from all over Asia as a celebration not only of their own culture, but also Japan, Korea, Vietnam, and other Asian countries. It's all part of the store's evolution as well as the Chen family's ability to adapt, which they've had to do multiple times over the years. People were worried the shop would close for good in 2015 when the owners of Pearl River's prior location raised the store's rent by an additional $6 million a year. The Chens appeared to be out of options, but they had family and a community they could depend on. Joanne, the daughter-in-law of Mr. and Mrs. Chen, was one of countless New Yorkers who didn't want to see the business end, so she stepped in and helped expand the store with more online presence, an outpost in the Museum of Chinese in America, a food spot at Chelsea Market, and

TIP

This is where I go when I want to buy a gift for someone who spends a lot of time in the kitchen. From chili crisp to black sesame paste, you could easily fill a small suitcase with the various sauces and oils they sell.

a branch in Tribeca, which unfortunately shuttered in 2021. Not long after that, Pearl River was back, better than ever, in SoHo. The new store celebrates the family and the area they've called home all these years, as well as the immigrant experience in the US.

"We're part of a big story," Joanne tells me. It's about Chinese Americans, but it's also about all the other people who have come here looking for a better life.

PUNJABI DELI

114 EAST 1ST STREET

 unjabi Deli is one of those little spots that is easy to overlook but is such an important part of New York. It was open 24–7 for years but had to cut back its hours during the COVID-19 pandemic. While hungry vegetarians were no longer able to grab some late-night chana masala, another portion of the population was affected as well: taxi drivers. My friend Jani, who opened Punjabi in 1993, counted himself among their ranks. He came to the United States from India's Punjab region. When he opened up shop, his top priorities were to make great food while providing a place for cab drivers to relax.

Slowly, a big part of that customer base has gone away, but Punjabi has been such a vital part of the neighborhood for so long that new generations will continue to discover it.

"I know most of the customers who come here personally and as friends, but a lot of my old taxi driver customers don't come in here anymore. Many of the drivers died or retired," Jani says. Once the shutdown happened, with business down to nearly nothing, it was looking bad for one of my favorite places in Manhattan. Thankfully, enough people know and love Jani, his shop, and its delicious, inexpensive food. Customers new and old pitched in, raising over $50,000 to keep the beloved spot going.

> **Punjabi Deli has some of the best hot chai in the city. But don't expect any nut milk.**
>
> *TIP*

"In the beginning, I only had two things: spinach and chana masala," Jani says. Before he arrived, the space was a shop that fixed flat tires. "I came in, the rent was $700." And while finding rent like that anywhere in NYC is as close to impossible as it gets for a small shop, Jani still prices his food as though rent isn't a factor. At Punjabi, a bite to eat and a can of soda will set you back less than five bucks.

We love to toss around the word "hero," but I feel that Jani, and all the people in this book, are downright heroic for providing special spaces and services to New Yorkers. But there is something extra special about what Punjabi represents and the old New York City it connects us to.

RAY'S CANDY STORE

113 AVENUE A

Ray's is where you go if you crave fried Oreos, beignets dusted with powdered sugar, fries, milkshakes, and basically anything else your doctor tells you that you shouldn't have but makes you happy. All of it is served in a perfectly ramshackle little counter shop, the way things used to be in New York City.

People obsessed with Ray's are even more obsessed with the man it's named after. During the pandemic, with the bills mounting up, locals donated close to $50,000 to help the local legend keep the lights on. During some of the worst times in the city—the gritty 1970s, the Tompkins Square Riots of 1988, 9/11—he's always kept the lights on. No matter what time of day, people from nearby bars and punk clubs show up at his door looking for something to help relieve terrible hangovers, and he always delivers. Whether it's somebody needing something sweet after a bad

March 15 is National Egg Cream Day. No better place to spend the holiday than at Ray's.

breakup or a rough day at work, they know they can always stop in at Ray's and they'll be taken care of. They know they can count on him.

Born in 1933, Ray joined the Iranian Navy as a teenager, then left home for good after deserting during a tour of the East Coast. He made it to New York City in 1964, where he lived undocumented until he became a US citizen in 2011. In between that, he worked as a waiter, until one day he found out that a little candy shop was for sale in Alphabet City. He bought it and worked day and night to make ends meet while living upstairs, where he still resides. People love to talk about what makes a true New Yorker, but I don't know anybody who has the bona fides Ray's got.

Whenever I go in, there's always a mix of NYU kids, a few guys from the neighborhood with face tattoos and hardcore band T-shirts on, and usually some Japanese or German tourists who heard about the place through social media.

Ray is in his ninth decade, and he talks with them, gives directions, and even takes pictures with anybody who asks. The guy is a local celebrity.

Everybody should have a Ray's memory. Go in, talk to Ray, and let him tell you stories about his life in Iran or what the neighborhood was like twenty or thirty years ago, then order whatever you're feeling at that moment, whether it's a milkshake or a plate of cheese fries. Or just bask in the fact that you're in a really special place with one of the most beloved people in the city.

ROGUE

154 ALLEN STREET

Downtown has always been a place for scene-setters and tastemakers. In the 1980s, people started heading below 14th Street to figure out how to dress like Madonna, Fab 5 Freddy, or Cyndi Lauper; in the 1990s, it was people like Chloë Sevigny who everybody wanted to look like. In the new century, people across the globe were trying to look like the lost member of the Strokes. The young go Downtown both to be noticed and to notice others, and Emma Rogue is

hard to miss. That's why in 2021 a *New York Times* headline proclaimed, "It's Emma Rogue's Downtown Now."

Emma's a big reason why you see so many people remixing Y2K styles these days. Take the Spice Girls, Britney Spears, and early 2000s TRL, then mix them up with bits and pieces from other decades, and that sort of starts it off. But it's more nuanced than that. Emma has an incredible eye. The first iteration of her shop began in 2018 on Depop. Then her online presence

began to grow. "I was doing the whole street fair thing alongside that, and then I got on TikTok in 2020, and that boosted my sales." People looked to Emma for tips on how to dress, so giving them a place to shop for stuff she likes was next on her list. The thing is that Emma is a big dreamer and didn't want to limit herself to online sales; she wanted to do something IRL.

A year later, a few of her friends from the vintage world started opening shops in the city. This was 2021, one of the rare times in the last few decades when somebody could get a lease for cheap. While many thought the city was going to die during the pandemic, Emma decided to take a chance. A friend told her about a space on Stanton (she has since moved down the block to Allen Street). "I called the broker on Monday, signed the lease later that week, moved in May 15th, and opened on June 5th."

Things moved at lightning speed from there. No business plan, no concept, nothing. Just Emma's taste, personality, following, and a store full of vintage stuff that gets scooped up fast. "I had to do it. I *had* to! I had enough money in my bank account to pay for a year, and my lease was a year, so if I failed, I knew I could pay my rent for a year," she tells me.

Emma's got her own personal style, but the stuff she brings into the shop is all over the place. Neon green 1990s Nike tracksuits are displayed next to a Christina Aguilera tour shirt from 2001; Deadstock patchwork jeans next to a fuzzy pink dress that made its debut on a Paris runway in 1998; Rick Owens next to streetwear from the aughts, you name it. If Emma likes it, that's the big test. There's a reason it's her Downtown—she knows what's good.

TIP

Emma says that if you come to NYC and you want to shop for vintage, the Lower East Side has turned into "the vintage district." She says her store is one of a bunch you should check out. Also be sure to check out Bowery Showroom down the street. It sells a mix of new and vintage clothing, but the stuff on the new side is really a look at what's going to be cool in six months or so. The place serves as an incubator for young local designers to get their stuff seen.

MANHATTAN

75

RUSS & DAUGHTERS

179 EAST HOUSTON STREET

y friends from the Old Jewish Men collective like to kvetch about everything from how expensive lox is to the lack of public toilets in the city, which, to be fair, they're right about. Another thing they love to complain about is people who mistakenly call Russ & Daughters a Jewish deli. It's not. If you want that, you go to Katz's a few doors down. Russ & Daughters, the temple to herring and whitefish, is something totally different, and that's the first thing fourth-generation co-owner Josh Russ Tupper points out. "Appetizing. We're not a deli. A deli sells meat. We sell fish."

Selling fish is what the family has been doing for more than a century. Polish Jewish immigrant Joel Russ opened the doors at the original shop in 1920. His decision to get his three girls involved made it the first business in the United States to have "& Daughters" in its name. Joel, along with Hattie, Ida, and Anne,

TIP

Even though he has tried every conceivable combination in the store, when I ask Josh if he has a go-to order, he tells me it's a toasted bialy with melted butter and some pastrami lox on top—sounds pretty impossible to beat.

became famous for smoked sturgeon and schmaltz herring. Josh and his cousin Nikki Russ Federman have brought the store into the twenty-first century, even opening a café and satellite stores around the city.

While the other locations are great, there's something unique about the original Houston Street store. If you want a true New York City experience, get in there with the crowd, put in your order, and find somewhere to sit and eat.

"I think people are intimidated," Josh tells me. "Maybe it's the history or this idea that you need to know something, like some secret code. But the truth is that you should have an idea of what you want. Ask the person behind the counter what they'd suggest. They're here to help. They can tell you they get something with this sort of bagel or that kind of smoked salmon, or that they love your order, but they top it off with a little wasabi roe."

That's right. Let the slicers, the folks taking your order, be your guide. Spend enough time at Russ & Daughters and you realize the white-coat professionals behind the counter are some of the most chill people in the city.

While Russ & Daughters is famously "The House That Herring Built," there's way more than fish. The coffee is good, the pickles are delicious, and they also sell some of the best-looking tote bags around. Stuff one full of bagels, a thing of cream cheese, some whitefish salad, a little tub of the tuna salad Josh says people tend to overlook ("I eat that stuff a few times a week," he tells me), and maybe a loaf or two of babka for something sweet later. "We just want you to enjoy yourself," Josh says.

S&P LUNCH

174 FIFTH AVENUE

The iconic Flatiron lunch counter formerly known as Eisenberg's Sandwich opened in 1928 and became beloved for its tuna melts and Jewish deli sandwiches that would make your heart skip a few possibly unwelcome beats. Under various owners, it survived everything from world wars to 9/11. But when a For Lease sign went up in the window in 2021, the fear was that the pandemic was the one thing it couldn't survive.

Enter Matt Ross and Eric Finkelstein. When the owners of the Brooklyn sandwich shop Court Street Grocers heard that Eisenberg's was on the market, they decided to give it a shot. Eisenberg's was a place they loved going to when they were younger and starting out in the restaurant business; seeing it go away felt like something they just couldn't let happen.

"We had a friend who knew the broker, and he put in a word for us," Matt tells me as he takes a bite of the famous tuna melt sandwich the shop has long been known for.

"The original name was S&P," Matt says. When the pair got the lease, they dug

> **If it's cold and you're looking for something that will warm you up, look no further than "The Big Soup":** a matzo ball, kreplach, noodles, and chunks of flanken in chicken soup.
>
> *TIP*

into the archives and found that the place known for its delicatessen fare had a different name for a year or so until owner Monas Eisenberg renamed it after himself. Generations of New Yorkers shuffled in and out of Eisenberg's. It wasn't glamorous, trendy, or even that comfortable given the tight quarters at the counter (there are more spacious booths in the back), but that's what made it so great. So other than the name, Matt and Eric didn't want to change much else. What they did want to do was reintroduce the comfort food people expected when they walked into 174 Fifth Avenue, and maybe dial it up a notch.

"The last owners cut too many corners," one diner who's been eating there since the 1980s tells me. "Used to be the best tuna melt in the city. Then the last guy came in and something about it was off. These guys brought it all back."

Eric and Matt brought back a lot of the old menu, along with some former staff. The lady who greets you when you walk in has worked there for three decades, and some of the guys in back were making sandwiches when it was still Eisenberg's.

The menu is exactly what you want from a place with a long counter and a few tables in the back. A lot of artery-clogging deliciousness. The Reuben is great, and the Mel Brooks with corned beef, pastrami, turkey, mustard, Russian dressing, and coleslaw is insanely good. You can get chopped liver on iceberg lettuce with Saltines, and their plate of salami and eggs is the perfect morning starter. If you're watching calories, the melon with cottage cheese is an old-school favorite.

"This place is important to us," Matt says from across the counter. "We wanted to do it right," Eric adds as he hands a customer a bowl of matzo ball soup. When I ask the guy next to me, who's been coming for years, how he thinks they're doing, he smiles.

"This place is in its golden age! Best it's been since I started coming, and I was here back when Ed Koch was mayor. You know how long ago that was? A long time! This place was here way before then, and it's here now because New York needs places like it."

He's right.

SWEET PICKLE BOOKS

47 ORCHARD STREET

I had one chance to do this, so I did it," Leigh Altshuler says about why, in November 2020 of all times, she decided to open not just a used bookstore, but a used bookstore *and* pickle shop.

Leigh saw an opportunity while everybody else was trying to get out of the city. But New York was her home, so if she wanted to open the store of her dreams, there was only one place to do it. She found a space on the Lower East Side and decided to focus on two things: "Used books and pickles," she says confidently.

Leigh is part of a long tradition of New Yorkers who turned a unique vision into a reality. Combining pickles and books isn't the most intuitive business plan, but that's

why it's brilliant. People love both things, so naturally people are going to talk about a place that brings them together. That's why the tight store is usually packed with people looking to leave with a vintage paperback and a jar of brined cucumbers.

When you look at the history of NYC, the best things often come out of the worst times. It sounds clichéd, but it's the truth. New Yorkers are proud of how people in this city figure out a way to make it through tough economic times like the 1970s or after the attacks on September 11, 2001. During another bleak period, Leigh gave people something to smile about. Now her store is a vital part of the downtown community.

"Some days we sell more pickles than books," she tells me. "At first I thought a few hundred jars would last me a year or two, but we sold all of those in a few months."

People bring in boxes of books all the time, and Leigh tells them she can't pay for them. "But most of the time they tell me they just want some pickles, so I'll give them some."

You could devote an entire weekend to shopping New York's bookstores: The Lit Bar in the Bronx is great, Astoria Books in Queens is beloved by locals, Unnameable in Prospect Heights has one of the best used selections around, and at least a dozen other places all over town have become vital community spaces. Bookshop culture is one of the best things about New York, and Leigh is part of it. But the difference between Sweet Pickle and other indies is that Leigh figured out a different way to get books into people's hands. It's a book and pickle shop, but it's also a tribute to the history of the neighborhood where Jewish immigrants from Eastern Europe used to set up on the sidewalk selling everything from bagels to fish to, yes, pickles.

"I'm selling the two things I love," she says.

> **TIP**
>
> Orchard Street is a gold mine for great food and shopping. Make an afternoon of it by hitting LAAMS for great art, books, and clothing; Leisure Centre for awesome vintage; Beverly's for home and kitchenware; and Regina's for my favorite Italian sandwiches in the neighborhood.

THE SOCK MAN

99 ST. MARKS PLACE

St. Marks used to be the drag in Manhattan for all things weird and underground. Things have changed. The crust punks aren't begging for change as much and the record stores have been largely replaced by bars and restaurants, but Marty Rosen, the Sock Man, remains. You can't miss him—he looks like he could be the fifth Ramone.

Marty's shop used to be located down the block during the last great St. Marks era. Along with punkwear emporium Trash & Vaudeville, and record shops like Kim's Video and Sounds, it made St. Marks the destination if you wanted to find, well, basically anything. All those places ended up closing or moving, but Marty

TIP

Despite what you've maybe heard about Marty being "The Grumpiest Man on Earth," according to the *Daily News*, he can actually be pretty nice . . . if he's in a good mood.

stuck around until 2016, when his landlord realized they could make way more money for the prime piece of real estate. So Marty packed up his socks and started looking for a new space. Thankfully, somebody on the block knew that Marty's shop served as a St. Marks anchor, and it needed to continue to live there.

Marty is from the old-school days when people peddled everything from books to antiques on Manhattan sidewalks. When Marty decided he wanted something a little more indoors, he asked himself, "What is something everybody needs?" The answer became his life's work.

Marty doesn't sell just any socks. Higher quality is what he looks for. Marty deals

with certain sellers and is picky about what he carries. Quality, but also socks that will stand out. You can buy socks of any color, socks covered in monkeys or pot leaves, socks that say "I love pickles" or ones that have yellow cabs on them.

KISS socks? He's got those. Socks with just about any breed of dog? Yup. Socks with little green aliens, the American flag, Botticelli's *Birth of Venus*, or anything else you could ever imagine on a pair of socks, Marty is and hopefully will forever be your guy. People go to the Sock Man and have a good time doing something that is almost always boring, but Marty seems to have cracked the code on that.

TING'S GIFT SHOP

18 DOYERS STREET

My pal China Mac took me to Ting's for the first time recently. Even though I had passed by thousands of times, I had never gone inside. I truly don't know what took me so long. It's incredible. Like so much of classic Chinatown, Ting's looks like it was frozen in another era. In this case, the middle of the twentieth century, but the little red shop could be even older. All owner Eleanor Ting

knows is that her family has been running the shop since 1958, selling everything from bamboo back scratchers to cotton jackets from China. The store has stayed true to its origins, selling Chinese goods that people in the local community and tourists alike want.

But there's another reason Ting's is significant. The place where it sits, on the corner of Pell Street and Doyers, feels like the neighborhood crossroads. Look in any direction and you'll see see Chinese lettering, restaurants, beauty salons, and little shops run by locals, some of whom have been in the neighborhood for decades. Outside of Ting's, Doyers Street is

discrimination against them and other Asians. When the Chinese Exclusion Act was passed in 1882, Doyers and surrounding streets were among the few places

TIP

When visiting this location, you are right on the corner of arguably one of the most photographed streets in NYC. But many people don't know that Doyers Street (also known as the Bloody Angle) saw more gang-related murders in the early 1900s than any other intersection in the United States. Not exactly a tip, but just keep that in mind while taking your selfie.

people from China and of Chinese origin felt safe, not just in New York, but other places in America too. The local population grew again after the Immigration and Nationality Act of 1965 was passed, and the neighborhood has had to balance growth and gentrification since then. And in 2020, the first year of the COVID-19 pandemic, the neighborhood was gripped with fear again. Attacks against Asian Americans across the city, combined with so many businesses being forced to close, made people wonder if Chinatown would ever be the same.

Things gradually returned to some sense of normal. People are out walking around, fish is being delivered to nearby markets, and the sound of mahjong tiles can be heard clicking and clacking once again. Many people actually visit Chinatown just so they can learn to play the game, and China Mac tells me the best place to get a starter set is this little red shop. So if you're looking to pick up a new hobby, Ting's just might have what you're looking for.

closed to traffic, so you can sit at one of the tables where trucks and cars used to rumble down and take a few minutes to appreciate the sights and sounds of one of the best neighborhoods in the city. These days, when you look up, you can see buildings; but up until the middle of the twentieth century, there were elevated subway tracks above the street.

But the neighborhood's history goes back even further. New York's Chinatown dates back to the 1850s, and for the rest of that century and well into the next one, it served as a haven for the Chinese population after decades of racial

TOY TOKYO

91 SECOND AVENUE

When I was a kid and deserved a reward, there were a select few places my parents would take me. Forget the chain stores with their boring action figures you could get anywhere else; my dad took me to the small but carefully curated toy stores downtown. And Toy Tokyo was a favorite.

"I learned that through it all, good times or bad, whether there's money or it's a recession, people always want to buy what makes them happy," owner Lev Levarek tells me.

Before he started Toy Tokyo in the early 2000s, Lev collected old Japanese robots. He even lived in Japan for a while. "I went to all the shops in Tokyo, in Osaka, all over," he says. "I wanted to open up something similar, and we did." You can get anime stuff downstairs, and there's no shortage of stuff from Japan. There are also entire cases filled with Funko Pop figurines and action figures from popular 1970s and '80s movies like *Jaws* and *Ghostbusters*. The place is nerd paradise, but one thing in particular made Toy Tokyo popular.

"We are, how can I say, the representatives for after-market KAWS collectibles. Basically, whoever buys

TIP

You're right down the street from Veselka and B&H Dairy if you want something to eat. If you want to catch a flick you probably won't see playing anywhere else, Anthology Film Archives is also nearby.

KAWS from us sees an appreciation. What we were selling back in the day for $350 now sells for ten thousand dollars."

Today, KAWS is compared to greats like Andy Warhol and is exhibited in museums all over the world. Lev appreciated KAWS's work before just about anyone else did, and he's proven over and over that he's got a great eye for what's cool that will also make a great investment.

I was probably eleven or twelve the first time I went to Toy Tokyo. It was actually my dad who got me hooked. I realize now that he took me there to satisfy his own obsession: miniature plastic furniture. Now I understand why. Toy Tokyo is its own little world. For Lev, it's bigger than toys.

"I get to bring people joy," he says. "I wouldn't want to do anything else."

VESELKA

144 SECOND AVENUE

It's hard to overstate how important Veselka has been to downtown Manhattan since it opened in 1954. The beloved Eastern European comfort food spot had always been a destination for everybody, from the breakfast and lunch crowds to the NYU students cramming at two in the morning to the after-hours party people showing up after the bars close in search of fortifying starch. But in February 2022, when Russia invaded Ukraine, things took on an even deeper meaning. Third-generation owner Jason Birchard realized the East Village diner was part of a community extending far outside of Manhattan, and the United States as well.

"It became a hub. It makes sense in a lot of ways just because of where we are,

TIP

Don't sleep on the lime rickey. A New York classic, Veselka makes one of the best.

the community around us, the sort of food we serve. But it was really incredible in the middle of this terrible time to see all these people coming together," he says of the way the local community found a connection back to their Ukraine family and friends through Veselka.

"Veselka" means rainbow in Ukrainian. And it's beautiful to walk in and see a rainbow of people from every walk of life. Veselka was already a community within a community. But it was also part of another community, the Little Ukraine neighborhood, which includes other great restaurants such as the Ukrainian East Village Restaurant a few doors down, St. George Ukrainian Catholic Church, and the Ukrainian Museum.

Eat varenyky (pierogies) at Veselka, and you're sitting in the middle of so much New York City history, from Patti Smith giving poetry readings across the street at St. Mark's Church, to the Yiddish Walk of Fame in front of a bank that was once the iconic 2nd Ave. Deli (before it was forced to move uptown due to a rent hike).

Jason knows he's upholding a legacy. From Ukrainian sausages to stuffed cabbage, Veselka is still a place people go to because everything is great. Some say they have the best potato latke in the city. But they're probably most famous for their borscht.

Like everywhere else, Veselka suffered through the pandemic and the restaurant shutdowns in 2020. But as Jason says, "The community was here. Both New Yorkers along with people outside the city ordered from us online. It was tough, but you learn how good people can be during the hardest times."

Two years later, he saw it again. This time it was Veselka supporting its community by raising funds for Ukraine, redoing the black-and-white cookie with the blue and yellow of the Ukrainian flag, or just serving soup or dumplings to refugees and immigrants to remind them of home. Veselka once again took on new meaning to the people of the community.

VILLAGE REVIVAL RECORDS

197 BLEECKER STREET

Despite being notoriously tight on space, New York is a city for collectors. Books, vintage clothes, old toys from any era. You name it and it's likely you can find it here. But the classic, humble record shop has mostly faded away. Gone are iconic spots like Bleecker Bob's and Other Music, where record obsessives could spend hours looking through thousands of old LPs for that one gem. Village Revival Records, thankfully, remains.

"It's a part of the culture," my friend Jamal Alnasr says. Walking around his shop is every music nerd's dream. It's crammed with vinyl, CDs, some scattered old DVDs, and music memorabilia like a vintage Talking Heads poster from the 1970s for which people have offered Jamal insane amounts of money. It's the sort of place where you really have to undertake; the kind of old-school crate-digging that will yield things like a Japanese version of a Frank Sinatra record or a DVD of Yanni *Live at the*

Acropolis as well as old disco singles, and rare seven-inch punk sides. "People who live in New York or visit are curious," says Jamal. "They like to find things. You can come here looking for something and you might find it, but you can also be surprised." Jamal is one of the kindest people I know, and also one of the city's great music lovers.

Jamal was a fan of the pop music he heard on a little radio he owned as a kid growing up in Palestine. But when he got to New York as a teenager and started working at his uncle's record store, he realized he actually knew very little about music. The only way to fix that, he figured, was to learn everything. And I mean *everything*. Rap, jazz, indie, whatever. Whenever I visit, he fills me in on everything from the connection between Jeff Buckley, Elliott Smith, and Nick Drake to Taylor Swift fans looking for rare singles.

Jamal's excitement is part of why people love Village Revival. Jamal is a fan, and fans are the people who buy records. The business has had plenty of ups and downs, especially once streaming came into the picture, and Jamal has had to weather business storms more times than he can count. But he loves what he does. Anyone who has 320,000 LPs and 650,000 CDs between the shop and his storage space would have to. But for Jamal, Village Revival is about more than the music. It's about the community he's become part of and the friends he's made over the more than thirty years he's been in business. "This is the best city in the world and I get to do this," he says. "I see the joy on faces all the time and I'm lucky, man."

> **TIP**
>
> **Check out Artful Posters just across the street. It's where I get all my art framed, and it's where every NYU college student goes when they move to the city and decorate their dorm room or first apartment. And you can't stop by Village Revival without getting coffee from Porto Rico a few doors down. The best cappuccino in the city, in my opinion.**

VILLAGE WORKS

12 ST. MARKS PLACE

I'm really lucky that I was raised by parents immersed in the arts. My mom, Louise Fili, is a graphic designer, and my dad, Steven Heller, has been an art director, editor, and writer. I got to experience so much because of them. And because of my dad, I have a connection to the city's long tradition of underground artists and publications. He wrote about it in *Growing Up Underground: A Memoir of Counterculture New York*. Read it and you'll get a glimpse into the way New York City used to be—a place where artists, writers, and other outsiders could live and create. Artistic people still live and create here, but

it used to be easier when rents weren't as astronomical as today. A place like Village Works gives me hope that there is still some connection to that past and things will be better in the future.

Joseph Sheridan made his way from LA to Manhattan in 1983. That was the era you often read about when bands like Talking Heads and artists like Jean-Michel Basquiat paid next to nothing for huge Soho lofts. Meanwhile, a large pool of painters, poets, and punks were concentrated in downtown areas like the Lower East Side. That's where Joseph gravitated. During the 1990s, Joseph promoted a weekly Sunday nightclub party called Cafe con Leche, known for its reflection of NYC culture and diversity. In

They're always hosting readings and art shows. Stay up-to-date by following Village Works on Instagram.

TIP

2020 Joseph took over a space on Third Avenue for a reasonable price. That's where he opened the gallery, bookstore, and artist hangout known as Village Works. There he joined forces with poet-artist twins Damian and Dominic. They were homesick for the pregentrified city they were born into, connected immediately with the authenticity of the store; and they also brought current youth culture into Village Works. The first obstacle for the three was that the good rent didn't last long, and in spring 2023, Village Works relocated to a new space on a stretch of NYC that has always had a special place in the hearts of artists from Andy Warhol to the New York Dolls: St. Marks Place.

What makes Village Works more than just another great bookstore is how it feels like it could have existed during any era, whether it was the hippies and radical poets from the 1960s, the Patti Smith and Ramones crowds of the 1970s, the hardcore kids and performance artists of the 1980s, or any other group of weirdos who'd be considered legends today. Village Works specializes in zines and indie press books by writers who have a connection to the area, from the poetry of Allen Ginsberg to short story collections by Lynne Tillman and Ada Calhoun's book about the street where the shop is located, *St. Marks Is Dead*. It's NYC-specific in a not-corny way. Many of the flyers on the wall are drawn by hand, the way people used to do for parties and CBGB matinee shows. It looks and feels like what people mean when they bring up "Old New York," except it's now and always full of new stuff to experience.

YU & ME BOOKS

44 MULBERRY STREET

There are the daily headaches small business owners deal with, and then there are nightmare scenarios they try not to think about until actually confronted with them. Lucy Yu was forced to deal with the latter when a fire tore through her Chinatown bookstore and café on July 4, 2023. "Everything was pretty much ruined," Lucy says. "We had to gut everything." But she wasn't going to call it there. "We rebuilt a bookstore in a temporary space in two and a half weeks."

In just under a month, Yu & Me Books was rebuilt. She didn't even take a breath. "I'm a first-generation American," she continues. "There's just no option to give up or stop, because my parents didn't give up to get here."

Yu & Me carved out an important place in the city from the start when it opened in late 2021. At the time, New York was experiencing a spike in anti-Asian hate crimes, and Lucy—whose background is in chemical engineering—felt the need to do something. Opening Chinatown's first Asian American bookstore was the answer.

There's
something
symbolic about
New York's
Chinatown getting
a bookstore
that focuses
on literature by
immigrant authors, writers of color, and
especially Asian American novelists, poets,
and memoirists. Pulitzer Prize–winner Hua
Hsu, bestselling musician Michelle Zauner,
and the author and civil rights lawyer Qian
Julie Wang are a few of the people for
whom Yu & Me has hosted events. It's also
a great place to buy books and just chill out
for a second.

So would Lucy consider franchising
Yu & Me? Maybe opening them all over the
country?

"No," she says with a laugh. "One is
enough for me."

TIP

Lucy loves eating in
the neighborhood and
recommends Miss Du's
for its mango pomelo
sago drink. She also
stops by Art Bean for
house-roasted coffee.
And while you are on
this Chinatown food
tour, stop by one of my
favorite spots for cheap
eats, May Wah.

And the city responded from the start. Yu
& Me hosted packed events and built up
a dedicated base of customers while also
turning into a place bookish out-of-towners
heard they needed to check out. The fire
will forever be a part of the shop's story, but
more because of how its owner responded
to it by getting right back to work.

There was a time when you'd tell somebody in Manhattan you were going to Brooklyn and they'd look at you as if you were about to visit another continent. Now you're as likely to hear that somebody from Manhattan is moving to Brooklyn as the other way around. But there's a lot of ground to cover when you start talking about the borough that gave us Spike Lee, Nathan's Famous hot dogs, and where the Dodgers broke the racist color barrier when they signed Jackie Robinson to play at Ebbets Field in 1947.

Brooklyn is huge, with 2,736,074 residents. Manhattan, just to compare, has an estimated 1,694,250. You could take all the people who live in Saint Lucia, Grenada, Micronesia, Tonga, Greenland, and Monaco, and they still would make up only about a quarter of Brooklyn's population. Brooklyn was its own city until 1898, so if somebody were to suggest that Brooklyn break off and become its own state, it might seem far-fetched, but it's got the numbers.

Covering it all can be a trek. It takes at least an hour to get from Williamsburg or Bushwick to Coney Island, and there's an entire neighborhood called East New York. There's a *lot* of Brooklyn. Cultures within the cultures flourish there, from Park Slope parents to the various Hasidic Jewish or Caribbean groups in the central part of the borough, not to mention Sunset Park's Chinatown or the Italian communities that have called the same neighborhoods home for generations. Like anywhere else in the city, it's impossible to fully comprehend everything about Brooklyn. And that's what makes it great.

You can read any number of books about how important Brooklyn is to New York and America, but to really get just how great it is, you need to see for yourself—from Little Caribbean and Coney Island to Prospect Park and Williamsburg. And that's just scratching the surface. Like every part of the city, I could list a hundred more recommendations for each borough if we had the space. But those I cover here serve as a good starting point.

ALLAN'S BAKERY

1109 NOSTRAND AVENUE

The Caribbean community around Flatbush, Church, Nostrand, and Utica avenues in Brooklyn has been growing since the late nineteenth century. That's why my friend Shelley Worrell worked so hard to get the neighborhood named Little Caribbean. So when she tells me the spots she thinks truly represent her part of town, it's no surprise that one of them has been serving the community for almost as long as the community has existed.

Allan's Bakery opened in 1961. Before then, owner Christian Smith's grandparents sold hard dough bread and other pastries out of their station wagon at cricket and soccer matches. "They'd bake in their tiny oven at home after they got off work, and eventually, they were able to open their first storefront, and then they heard about

Give the bread pudding a shot. It's unlike any other you've ever had.

TIP

this one," Christian tells me as we watch a group of workers prep dough in the back. Everything baked at Allan's is part of a very long and ongoing story, one that really feels representative of the neighborhood itself.

"My grandfather came from Saint Vincent, and his parents are from there and also Trinidad," Christian adds, but that's only part of the story. "My grandmother came from Panama, but her parents are from Jamaica and India." To show how deep his roots go, he mentions that he even had a great-grandfather who came from Aruba. Every part of Allan's Bakery has some story that traces back to somewhere else, especiallly the food. They serve coconut buns and tamarind balls, cakes with mango filling, and even savory foods like codfish patties and beef roti. But if there's one thing they're especially famous for, it's their currant rolls.

"They're the most popular item," Christian says. His blend of currants, sugar, and spices wrapped in puff pastry are the result of a multipart process involving at least two bakers. How currant rolls became a Caribbean favorite isn't totally known, but Christian says a popular theory is that they're related to the Eccles cake from the UK, which traveled overseas with immigration, "and then people in the Caribbean did their own takes on it."

Even though they cater to people from all over the West Indies, and the family's own lineage goes back to several parts of the region, Christian says that since the beginning, Allan's Bakery knew exactly what it was. "We just say we're a Caribbean bakery," Christian says with a smile.

ANTHONY & SON PANINI SHOPPE

433 GRAHAM AVENUE

If there's such a thing as New York Nico HQ, this is it. Anthony & Son is an institution among the Italian American community around the edge of Williamsburg right by the BQE. That's not only because Anthony and his family make some of the best sandwiches in Brooklyn, but also because they represent a bridge between the Italian American community's past, present, and future.

That and the really great sandwiches.

My connection to the place started in December 2016. I got an Instagram message from the shop telling me I had posted a picture of a crossing guard on Graham Avenue, who turned out to be the aunt of the person running their account. I had been to the Panini Shoppe once or twice before, and was getting more in touch with my Italian roots, so I thought I should connect with them. I was also doing a clothing drive, and I asked if they'd be willing to donate sandwiches. It wasn't until I was hanging out there one night, and was

NEW YORK NICO'S GUIDE TO NYC

TIP

Anthony & Son recently added outdoor seating due to popular demand, so if it's a nice day and you have the time, sit down for a meal rather than getting the food to go. Also, they make a few sandwiches on garlic bread. If you're a fan, I highly recommend trying one. Unless you've got a date later on. Your breath isn't going to smell great for at least five to eight hours.

introduced to my friend Charlie the Wolf, that I realized something about the place made it a farm system for New York's most interesting people. After years of stopping in on an almost daily basis, it now feels like I'm visiting family.

When you enter, you can't miss Anthony, the owner. He's the guy wearing the iced-out Panini Shoppe chain. He came to New York in 1988 from Salerno, Italy. After realizing landscaping wasn't for him, he decided to open an eatery in 1994. "When

you're an immigrant, you don't have a lot of choices," Anthony says. "There's only so much work available to you." Back when they started, the store was much smaller. At one point, Anthony had his family making fresh pasta by hand, which they sold in sandwich bags for a dollar each. Eventually, the focus turned to sandwiches.

Anthony and his wife Teresa's kids, Sabino and Michela, further helped bridge the gap between Italy and twenty-first-century America. If you've followed me for a bit, you know Sabino has been a huge part of what I've tried to do over the last few years. The kids have gotten their parents on social media, they design merch that shows up in fashion magazines, and Sabino hosts his popular *Growing Up Italian* podcast

grilled chicken, pepper jack, avocado, crispy onions, and chipotle mayo is damn good. And if you're a little Anthony Soprano and want some baked ziti, it's a sleeper hit.

If you stop by when Anthony or any of his family are hanging outside, you'll notice most locals say hello. I once asked them why they thought everybody knew them. Now I know the answer. They own a great sandwich shop and people love great sandwiches, but Anthony adds that isn't so easy to pull off in a place like New York, where things change quickly. "They know us. They know we're here, and they care because we care."

upstairs. The whole family cares about where they came from, but also where they're at, so their shop has become a hub for Italian Americans. I've met everybody from Cugine, to Erma, to Big Joe Gambino through the Panini Shoppe.

An even bigger part of my story is how much weight I've gained eating at Anthony & Son. I can't tell you how many times I've told people to meet me there and they'll ask me what to get. I have my favorites, but the truth is that whatever they order, they can't go wrong. Try the FDNY hero, a chicken cutlet topped with vodka sauce and fresh mozz served on garlic bread; or their eggplant parm if you don't want meatball. And, if I may, the New York Nico wrap with

THE BAKERY ON BERGEN

740 BERGEN STREET

There's a real premium on quiet places in New York City. You either get used to the noise or you don't; but a chill, relaxing spot that takes you out of the grind for a little while is something you can really learn to appreciate. That's why I think classic bakeries, the type that serve colorful cupcakes, cookies with big chocolate chips, and a good cup of coffee, become so beloved. A few are scattered throughout the city. Some get famous (like Magnolia Bakery in the West Village), but most are important local spots for people who live in, or visit, the neighborhood.

The Bakery on Bergen is a prime example of the latter. It's a quiet little spot where I can get my favorite peanut

Everything tastes good, but the peanut butter cookie is my favorite thing on the menu. They also switch up cupcake flavors seasonally.

TIP

butter cookies, and it's just hidden enough that it feels like a nice little secret, but it has thrived as the neighborhood around it continues to grow. It serves a purpose just like the nearby diners, bodegas, or family-owned grocery stores. It's not just a business—it's part of the community.

That was important to Akim Vann. She wanted it to be a bakery *for* the neighborhood because she's *from* the neighborhood. She grew up nearby and saw that a bakery can serve as important a role as any other local establishment. But it took some time for her to figure out that serving cookies and cupcakes was her calling.

"For a really long time, I knew I wanted to have my own space," Akim says. "I didn't necessarily know what that would be. I did have an idea for a cooking school for children a long time ago, and I actually do match-and-baking classes here."

Akim is a renaissance woman. She's a baker and a mathematician. That might seem like a strange leap, but when you consider that baking is all about measurements, numbers, and variables, being a math wiz probably helps. But for Akim, it's bigger than that. She sees her baked goods as a way to get people talking, and to invest in their neighborhood. It's sort of a genius move when you think about it.

The thing I like the most about Akim is how she keeps it all about the neighborhood. When I ask about the street her bakery is located on, she says a lot of people from out of town show up to try her stuff, but she doesn't want them to simply get something from the bakery and then get back on the train. "I feel like there's a bit of a domino effect here also, because I can tell you where to go to get a good sandwich. I can tell you where to go to get good seafood. I can tell you where to go hang out at night." In other words, you gotta do the whole neighborhood.

BULLETPROOF COMICS

2178 NOSTRAND AVENUE

You know how every great superhero has an origin story? The guy behind the counter at Bulletproof Comics has a story that could be straight out of the mind of Jack Kirby or Stan Lee. You may be thinking about the annoying Comic Book Guy from *The Simpsons*. Hank Kwon is a comic book guy, but he's not *that* Comic Book Guy.

"It used to be pretty dangerous back in the day," Hank, wearing a Mets shirt, tells me as he leans up against a poster of the Joker. He's describing this neighborhood as it was in the early 1990s when he opened his one-stop shop for all things comics, fantasy, and video games. Bulletproof is located in an area that brushes up against Flatbush and Midwood, and was a popular target for kids to show up and steal whatever they could get their hands on.

"These kids were about fifteen or sixteen. A few of them would come in after school, and they were picking on the younger kids. They were doing what was called 'running the pockets,' going through and taking what the kids had in their pockets. I wasn't going to stand for that, so I told them to stop. They wouldn't stop, so I kicked the guys out. They came back with seventeen guys, a little bit older, and were going to bum-rush the store. If they did that, the whole place would be demolished.

Somehow, we managed to convince them to take it outside."

What happened after that became the stuff of local legend. Hank, an immigrant from South Korea, continues: "I kicked one guy in the head with a roundhouse. And then everybody stopped and talked among themselves, and they left. That was the moment we earned our street cred. Those kids came back every day after that and were quiet as mice. They became customers. A lot of them are MTA workers today."

The last bit, about the kids who were trying to start trouble at the local comic shop growing up to become the people who drive city buses and fix subway tracks, highlights a bigger point about the importance of a place like Bulletproof Comics. Once they got past being jerks and started respecting Hank, the kids had a place to go. Bulletproof is an independently owned business, a place where local kids have gone for decades to stretch their imaginations and get inspired, all because Hank is on top of things and gets the best stuff. As I listen to his story, I'm surrounded by people of all ages. One of them, a guy who can't be more than eighteen years old, tells me there are other comic book shops in the city, but none of them does it like Hank. "He's a legend," he says. "I grew up coming here and I've learned everything from Hank. I used to be a comics guy, but

then I got into anime because he turned me on to that stuff."

And comics are far from the only thing Bulletproof specializes in. Hank also sells rare comic and fantasy art by DC and Marvel artists, skateboards, vintage video games, graphic novels, anime, and basically everything else good with which to fill your mind.

Hank takes his in-store comics signings very seriously. I am very impressed by the authors and artists he brings into his shop. Check out bulletproofcomix.com for a schedule of signings.

TIP

CIRCO'S PASTRY SHOP

312 KNICKERBOCKER AVENUE

Bushwick is another neighborhood about which people seem to have a lot of misconceptions. It's true that when Williamsburg started getting too expensive for artists and musicians, some folks moved a few stops east on the L train, from Bedford to Montrose. And just as in Williamsburg and Greenpoint, luxury apartment buildings started going up, and so did a lot of new businesses. But you'll still find a lot of the culture that made Bushwick great just by walking around, from excellent Dominican food at nondescript bodega hot bars to unique surprises, such as Maria Hernandez Park,

which is great. And then there's Circo's Pastry Shop, the bakery that has served as a crossroads for generations of people who have called Bushwick home.

The guy who brings them all together is Nino Pierdipino, a Sicilian immigrant who started working for the original Circo family in 1968, two years after coming to the United States. More than thirty years later, Nino and another baker bought the business from their old boss, with Nino eventually becoming the sole owner.

"I love to come here," he tells me before turning to a kid who is no older than five and asking, "You wanna come work for me? I'm tired."

If you want to get wild, get their "family size" cannoli—it's as big as a football.

TIP

These days, Nino's sons, Salvatore and Anthony, work with him at the bakery, ensuring Circo's will be around for a long time to come. The brothers both attended the Culinary Institute of America, and when I ask Anthony if his time there taught him anything that he's brought back to his family's bakery, he replies, "Probably," then looks around and adds, "but you can't really add anything to this, because it's years of work perfecting these recipes."

Circo's is best known for cakes. They're like the OG Cake Boss. Circo's does all kinds of crazy designs that would make the Cake Boss bow down, and it's the reason anyone planning a wedding or baptism around Bushwick keeps ordering from them. My friend Erma is a big fan of Circo's. The first time she took me there, I decided that something big and overly sweet might not be the right move, so I went with some handmade biscotti. A lot of people have told me about Circo's take on the famous Italian biscuits. They're the real deal, nothing like the prepackaged stuff at Starbucks. I took one bite, and as soon as the almond flavor hit my mouth, I saw something else I wanted to try, then something else, then another thing.

Later, as I stood on the sidewalk looking at the iconic old neon Circo's sign, I couldn't help thinking that nothing beats a good Italian pastry in Brooklyn. I hope everybody gets to experience it.

CLOUDY DONUT

14 COLUMBIA PLACE

I'm a born-and-raised New Yorker, but I understand that people who come here and contribute to the city being a better place are just as important as people who can claim day-one status. This is especially true when it comes to donuts. You want to move here to make music or art, go to NYU, or you want to become a Broadway star, be my guest; but if you move to New York City and want to add to the map of donut spots, you really need to bring something special to the conversation.

Cloudy Donut started in Baltimore, Maryland, before opening a location in Brooklyn Heights in 2022. Derrick Faulcon can thank the legions of TikTok fans who

TIP

You're not far from the Brooklyn Historical Society. Eat a donut and burn off the calories by walking over to see what they've got on display. Or just take a stroll along the Promenade.

helped blow up the original spot, but the fact is, they make incredible donuts. That and they're 100 percent vegan. The absence of any animal ingredients doesn't have an impact on the taste, and if you've ever had a donut from some big chain, and they taste extra heavy, you can usually blame it on the butter, eggs, or milk. Cloudy doesn't use any of that stuff. Their donuts are so fluffy and light you can pretend it's perfectly okay to have another one.

Derrick is big on the philosophy of "reverse gentrification"—being a Black business owner who goes into an affluent white neighborhood and offers up an item locals get obsessed over. His hope is that will help bridge the gap between Black and white, rich and poor, and set an example for other Black entrepreneurs who want to build generational wealth.

Each week, Cloudy rolls out eight donut flavors. When I pull up on a sunny day, they've got piña colada, blueberry, peanut butter and jelly, and five others. I go with the PB&J and the blackberry mint mojito they're offering.

It makes sense. Brooklyn Heights is where rich people from Manhattan used to move to when they wanted to escape the city in the 1800s—it's considered one of the first suburbs in the US. Today, it's still a calm and beautiful part of the city, except now they have one of the best donut places you'll find anywhere.

CREST HARDWARE & URBAN GARDEN CENTER

558 METROPOLITAN AVENUE

Hardware stores are the unsung heroes in any community's ecosystem, and big-box stores have basically obliterated the mom-and-pops. That's one reason Crest Hardware is so important to its neighborhood. But it's more than just a place to buy a hammer and some nails.

"My father and uncle started it in 1962, where that smoke shop is now," owner Joe Franquinha says. "Their parents had just emigrated from Portugal." He was bopping around and working in hardware before he bought the shop." The original Crest was a half-hardware, half-general store that didn't have many customers. The owner

only turned the lights on when there was a customer in the store. Joe's dad told the guy he'd be interested in buying the place, and that was the start of things.

In the mid-1970s, they moved across the street. Originally, it was only the first three aisles you see when you walk in the store today. Since then, however, Crest sits in the center of the neighborhood that it has grown along with, counterbalancing the big glass condos and corporate businesses that have taken over the rest of Williamsburg.

"Back then, it wasn't like they were giving buildings away, but it was a lot easier to be here," Joe says. His family bought the

Seriously, go have a conversation with Finlay the parrot, and give Franklin the pig a pat.

TIP

building and some of the buildings around it. They expanded the hardware store and added a garden center, which, when you walk in from Metropolitan Avenue, feels like you've entered another realm. But Joe's family realized that in order to keep up with the changing neighborhood, they had to have a plan. "We've been able to adapt and move and speak to people with disposable incomes," Joe explains. "Because if we just served people who shopped out of necessity, unfortunately, if we're just selling a few screws and rolls of tape a day, we're not going to survive. So we really take the time to find great pots for plants, yard games, stuff for camping, all sorts of stuff." Crest is a hardware shop first, but they want you to be able to knock more than hardware items off your shopping list.

Walk to the back, and you'll meet Finlay the parrot; walk outside the garden center and you'll find a local celebrity, Franklin the pot-bellied pig. Yes, you heard me right: They have a very cute pig named Franklin that kids and adults alike love to say hello to. All of it works as a reminder that Crest is truly unique.

Despite knowing they could likely make big money renting the space, which is just a few feet from the L train, to big businesses, they know that would kill the balance they've helped cultivate. "It was always our goal to make sure we're not adding another Starbucks or something like that. I think people understand that if they're going to show up on this block and want to be a part of it, then there are certain responsibilities that come with it."

CUTS & SLICES

93 HOWARD AVENUE

Here's the thing about Randy Mclaren: He's different. He's not like other pizza makers. "What people don't know about me is that I'm allergic to shellfish. So any pizza you see here with shellfish on it, I had to try it, so I'd eat it, then start breaking out, run to the bodega to get some Benadryl, and get back at it." There's that, the whole putting his health and well-being on the line to make some of the most unique pizza in Brooklyn. But there's something else he points out. "You know a lot of Black pizza shop owners?"

He's got a point. And that's why, in 2018, Randy moved from being the guy whose business it was to find the best and most expensive sneakers for his A-list clients to changing the pizza game. Randy and his wife, Ashlee, are New Yorkers, and they love a good, classic slice as much as anybody. Cuts & Slices isn't far from where Spike Lee's fictional Sal's Pizzeria from *Do the Right Thing* was located, and there are nods and inspiration taken from classic joints like it, but this isn't a traditional pizza place. Randy and Ashlee wanted to make

something different, pizza good enough for a New Yorker's standards, but that also had a connection to his family's roots in Trinidad.

"I always had a passion for food," Randy says. "Before sneakers, I was in food, and I knew one day I was going to open up a restaurant. I didn't think it was going to be a pizzeria, but I wanted to bring back the pizza I grew up eating." The East Flatbush native says he wanted his culinary creations to have "Quality. That's first."

Randy makes one of the most interesting slices in the city: curry oxtail. Maybe others have tried it, but if they did, I can only assume it turned their pizza into a bread bowl, because curried oxtail can be sort of soupy. But not the Cuts & Slices version. Randy has some secret magic. He was able to make the kind of crust he wanted—the kind that doesn't hurt your jaw when you're eating it—and it somehow also holds the beef without going limp. It's a delicious modern miracle.

Even though word has caught on about the new Bed-Stuy pizza landmark, Randy is still humble. Once when I was talking to him outside the shop, a guy walked up to him to say thanks. "I appreciate that, bro. I drove from Philly to try this," the guy said. Randy seemed moved. People making a trip to try his pizza isn't a new thing, but it's something he can't get over. "I want to do some life-changing shit for people. That's the concept, you come in here and get two cuts, which equals one slice. So you might get the chopped cheese, but you can also get a chicken and waffle as your other cut. I just want to make sure you leave here

TIP

The sweet chili oxtail cut with a cut of the jerk shrimp is hard to beat. Also, they now have a Queens location.

knowing you ate some pizza that you can only get here."

Word has spread. Celebrities like Lil Uzi Vert, Lil Yachty, and Damson Idris are fans. So is Adidas. The shoe brand did a collab with Randy. And if you want a true NYC stamp of approval, when Desus Nice went on Jimmy Kimmel in 2022, he didn't bring pizza from his hometown in the Bronx—he brought it from Cuts & Slices.

DEFONTE'S SANDWICH SHOP

379 COLUMBIA STREET

t's not the easiest place to get to, but Red Hook is one of those neighborhoods everybody needs to experience at least once. It has the true, old-school industrial Brooklyn feel to it, with cobblestone streets and union workers walking around. They've been making their living in this neighborhood since long before Marlon Brando "coulda been a contender" in *On the Waterfront*, which was based on the lives of the dock workers who populated the area. Things have changed a lot with the arrival of Ikea, a Tesla dealership, and little boutiques, but there's still no other part of the borough like Red Hook, and there's no sandwich place like Defonte's.

On any given day at Defonte's, you'll walk into a rush of locals, firefighters, dock workers, and hard hats plastered with union decals. My friend Lil Mo Mozzarella usually knows everybody there. That's the thing with Mo: Maybe he's old friends with them, or maybe he just met them. The point is he talks the same to everyone. That goes a long way in all New York boroughs, but especially in a place like Defonte's, which has been serving up heroes since 1922. And

TIP

Keep in mind that if you're ordering a large, it's a *really big* sandwich. So maybe just get two smalls. More variety, and you'll likely have lunch and dinner taken care of. If you want to get all your meals out of the way, you're only a few minutes from one of my favorite burgers in all of NYC at Red Hook Tavern, as well as one of the best key lime pies I've ever tasted at Steve's Authentic Key Lime Pie.

Mo has been going there for a long time.

The place gets crowded, so study the menu while you wait in line so you're ready to order when you get to the counter. Some people get one of the sandwiches named after a beloved local, others will get the sandwiches with broccoli rabe on them (the Vinny D, with grilled Italian sausage topped off with ricotta and grated parmesean, or the Fire House Special, with roast pork, provolone, and fried eggplant). Others go for a classic cold hero with fresh mozz, cold cuts, and whatever else looks good.

You can get a perfect sandwich any time of day, but Lil Mo says you're extra lucky if you get there when they bring out a fresh tray of potatoes and eggs, baked together with a layer of mozzarella on top between sliced Italian bread. "There's nothing better than that," says Lil Mo. There's just one more important thing, and it's the brown glass bottle Lil Mo pulls out of the drinks fridge. "You gotta eat it with this," he says as he shows me a bottle of Manhattan Special, the locally made espresso soda that's been produced in Brooklyn since 1895.

Back in the day, there were many more Italian American sandwich spots like Defonte's around Red Hook, but they've mostly disappeared. Defonte's staying power is in the sandwich. The place started as a bodega, but the longshoremen began asking for something quick and easy to eat on their breaks or after they clocked out. Original owner Nick Defonte started making ham and cheese dressed with lettuce, tomato, and some olive oil. What started out as an idea to make a little extra cash turned into the center of the business, and more than a hundred years later, Nick's grandson, Nicky, is keeping the place in the family. Next in line is Nicky's son, Vinny. We're all the better for the fact that "Defonte's is always gonna be Defonte's," as Lil Mo Mozzarella puts it.

FANTASY EXPLOSION

164A DRIGGS AVENUE

Kevin Fallon has been one of my closest friends since 2010. He's always had a genuine interest in New York City. He started his vintage business in 2017, and when you step into his Greenpoint store, it doesn't take long to understand what his focus is.

"I started finding things from all these New York institutions when I was sourcing, all kinds of restaurants and theaters and museums, and other New York referential ephemera. It became the bulk of my collection."

Kevin has an eye for the good vintage merch people will pay top dollar for online.

The iconic *New York* magazine logo created by Milton Glaser on a T-shirt might sit next to a trucker hat from some long-gone diner that served people in Queens, or you might find something from some TV show that was filmed here, such as *Sex in the City* or *The Sopranos*. Shirts from the 2003 blackout, mugs with Al Hirschfeld illustrations, or subway series–era Yankees and Mets gear.

"We've also done some re-creations," he mentions. There's the classic five-panel Metropolitan Opera baseball cap that style guys all over have been obsessed with since Kevin put them out. "Then we did the

collection with Bloomingdale's based on souvenir hats from the eighties and nineties. I draw inspiration from these things that I think should really live another life."

The thing that separates Kevin from a lot of other vintage dealers is the philosophy he brings to how he curates his inventory. It isn't just cool old stuff. He goes for the things he knows will look dope, but more important, have meaning and emotional value.

"I think that everything good, as far as clothing and graphic T-shirts, has probably been done before," Kevin tells me. "There's something special and romantic about a good vintage shirt, especially one that pulls at your heartstrings in a specific way."

Kevin understands that New York City is a great place in the present, but that people who live here are always nostalgic for the past. Whether it's five, ten, or fifty years ago, there are certain things from the past that every New Yorker longs for. Maybe it's an old restaurant or a building that's not there anymore. Whatever it is, this is a city filled with nostalgia, and Kevin taps into that.

5TH AVENUE RECORDS

439 FIFTH AVENUE

Park Slope isn't exactly off the beaten path. It's one of the most popular neighborhoods in Brooklyn, with its brownstones and famous food co-op drama. So it might surprise some people when I tell them one of the best record stores in the entire city is on the neighborhood's main drag, hidden behind one of the weirdest facades in all of Brooklyn.

The record shop has been here since 1972—more than fifty years. In 2019, Ryan Romanski, who worked for the previous owner, took over the space that had slowly turned into this sort of beautiful, odd, cluttered shop of records, tapes, and CDs. But nobody seemed to buy much. The owners didn't really have direction or focus, and the place just sort of sat there, looking like any day it would just be gone and a bank or smoke shop would take its place. But the power of persistence paid off.

"I tried to buy it a few years earlier, but it didn't work out," Ryan says. "A couple of years ago the former owner decided he wanted to close, so he hit me up, but the owners of the building kept saying they didn't want a record store in there. So I kept calling to see what was going on. Then three days before the last owner was supposed to

and his crew are all-around music heads. He's a DJ, producer, and record-label owner. Ryan is one of those guys who can talk to you about Prince

TIP

If you can't make it to Park Slope, 5th Avenue Records has one of the best online stores I know of via the record sale site Discogs. Look up 5thAveRecordsNYC to get a sense of how hard Ryan and his crew go when it comes to digging up the best vinyl.

B-sides but also pull out some rare disco or rap LP you've never heard of, then pull out another record and say "Here's the sample for that track," and all of a sudden you've got a stack of albums you need to own. "You won't find a concentration of stuff like mine anywhere else," he says. "We cater to everything: jazz, funk, and soul. For new stuff, I've got a lot of house and electronic music, but I let customers tell me if there's something on their radar, I'll order it for them."

Record shops were once easier to find in New York, especially ones that had true music freaks running them. Ryan is doing something important, but his love for the place, and the fact that he can talk music all day, is infectious. It reminds me of the days when people used to go to Bleecker Bob's in the Village or the old Academy Records in Williamsburg to learn about music they didn't know about, and not from an algorithm on an app.

close, I hit them up one more time and they said no, they didn't want me to take over because I'd been nothing but rude to them, I yelled at them, and all this stuff."

Ryan isn't exactly rude, and I can't really see him raising his voice, so he knew something was up. He realized they thought he was the *other* guy who worked at the store. "Once they found out I wasn't the *other* guy, they told me I could have the spot." See? People say New Yorkers are mean, but the fact that Ryan's a good guy ended up being the reason there's still a record store on Fifth Avenue.

Origin story aside, 5th Avenue Records now is different from the old place. Ryan

FORTUNATO BROTHERS

289 MANHATTAN AVENUE

Erma is one of my friends who always gives it to me straight, but even she takes a second to respond when I asked her to name the best thing at her favorite bakery. "The sesame cookies, oh my God," she says. So that's her favorite? She doesn't say yes or no but keeps pointing. "The struffoli," she says as she clutches her heart. "Some people call them honey balls, but if you're from around here they're struffoli." So that's her favorite? "No," she says as she points toward these beautiful shell-shaped pastries filled with cream. Some people call them lobster tails, Erma says. "The

sfogliatella. The best of the best."

I get why it's hard to pick out just one thing. Immigrants from Naples, the Fortunato brothers Mike, Mario, and Sal saw an opportunity to start their own thing after years of hard work. The space they're still in today became available and they jumped at the chance,

TIP

You are a couple blocks away from Edith's, my favorite bagel shop in the area. I'd go there first, get a pastrami, egg, cheese, and latke on a plain bagel, as well as their famous iced cafe slushie, and then hit Fortunato's for dessert.

even though baking wasn't the trade they all knew. "My father was a tailor," Sal's son Biagio, who runs the day-to-day operations, tells me as he sets an espresso on the table. "They all had jobs around here, whether it was unloading boxes or cleaning dishes," but it was and always has been a family affair.

Today you can get a cannoli basically anywhere. But in 1976, in an Italian neighborhood like Williamsburg, you had to be really good or else you were going to go out of business. So that's what the brothers excelled at, "things people missed from Italy," as Sal puts it. "But in the last fifteen years or so we started adding things like red velvet cake or certain kinds of cookies," to appeal to the changing neighborhood.

The Fortunato bakery is entrenched enough in a great location that they could easily rest on their laurels, or cater to the new neighbors whose only connection to Italy or Italian American culture is Scorsese movies. But that's not what this place is

about. They are welcoming to everyone and have things Erma will always come back for, but also bake treats that appeal to people who just moved in. "That's the secret weapon," Biagio tells me. "I'm always getting people hooked on the Italian stuff. A guy comes in every day and orders a coffee and a croissant, sooner or later I'm gonna tell him to try a cannoli, on me. And then he's hooked."

GREENBERG'S BAGELS

1065 BEDFORD AVENUE

It's a trope how seriously New Yorkers take their bagels. But it's true. When people visit, they want to know what all the fuss is about, so they're always asking where the "best" bagel in the city is. That's an impossible question to answer. Maybe you're looking for a bigger bagel, or perhaps you like a chewier one. I've heard a dozen different arguments about the best pumpernickel bagel alone. If you want authentic, that will depend upon what your idea of authentic is. Bagels have been in the city since the second half of the nineteenth century, when Jewish immigrants from Poland sold them on the Lower East Side, and my guess is they've changed a lot since then.

Eventually, the popularity of bagels spread far and wide. Montreal has its own sweeter, chewier version; even LA has had a bagel boom in recent years. There are good bagel places all over the country and Canada, but the difference between places like Philadelphia, Chicago, or Miami and New York City is the choices we New Yorkers have. If you ask someone where to get a bagel, they'll likely tell you to walk a block or two at most. The problem is that some are great, some are meh, and some are just not worth your time. Some simply sell bagels because they're part of the New York diet, but a place like Greenberg's isn't going to mess around, because what they sell is in their name. My general rule of

thumb is that if a place is brave enough to tell you they sell bagels on the sign, then it's worth trying.

Thankfully, Julian Cavin, friend and co-owner of Greenberg's Bagels, didn't want to serve basic bagels. If he was going to get into the game, the bagels he made had to pass his very tough standards. "Bagels are my favorite food. If I go on vacation for two weeks, the last three days I'm sitting around thinking what my first bagel when I get back to Brooklyn is gonna be," he says. So he got together with Jamison Blankenship, and the two opened up Greenberg's in 2018 with the simple idea of serving great bagels. It quickly became an institution.

I met Julian when we were both teenagers. We didn't go to the same school, but I saw him around. He was that kid from Brooklyn who was always hustling, selling sneakers, DJing, throwing parties, whatever. Julian was the guy everybody needed to know. Greenberg's "is an extension of that hustle," he told me one morning when I rolled up for a breakfast sandwich.

Julian knows the bagel is part of the culture of his hometown, and he respects that. "Some people try to say it's the water, or it's this or that, but it's that all these bagel rollers learned from previous bagel rollers, and those rollers learned from previous ones. There's history here. It's technique."

While the bagel is the king of breakfast in New York, a close second would be the classic bacon, egg, and cheese, aka the BEC. Any bodega in the city worth its weight in loosies and shady THC products should be able to put those three ingredients between a sliced roll. So simple, so good. Greenberg's BEC, though, is on another level, with all the meat, cheese, and eggs they use coming from the iconic Cobble Hill butcher shop Paisanos. "We're not doing this in a bougie way, we just have better ingredients," says Julian, who goes with the everything bagel for his.

As for his opinion on the best bagel shop in the city, Julian doesn't play around. He doesn't even throw his store in the mix. He simply says, "There's a good bagel or there's a bad bagel—it's black and white. Simple."

TIP

If you want another coffee after your bagel, but also want somewhere to sit, Playground Coffee Shop is right across the street, and it's one of the best cafés/community spaces/bookstores in Brooklyn.

L'INDUSTRIE PIZZERIA

254 S 2ND STREET

If there's any one thing that connects every pizza place in Brooklyn, it's that the person who owns it is likely an obsessive. That obsession is usually bred through experience, from years of putting pie after pie in the oven and making sure every pie is as great as the last.

Almost. L'Industrie co-owner Massimo Laveglia is one of the exceptions. "The shop was already open. A French guy owned it. I was working as a server, and I took over the shop in 2017. But I never made pizza before."

Excuse me?

"I got the shop without knowing how to make pizza. I taught myself. I learned a little from the French guy who I took over from, watching YouTube, stuff like that. At first, it was really slow here. I was making twenty to thirty pies a day, so that was good learning. It was a good school for me to learn."

In 2018, Massimo decided to call a pizzamaker friend in Rome and had him come to the States to show him how to up his game. "And that's it." That same year, Nick Baglivo came on to help Massimo steer

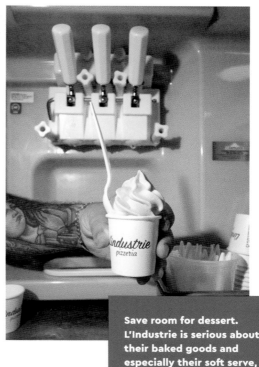

L'Industrie toward something more than just a slice shop, and things started taking off. These days, if you don't time things right, you're going to be waiting for your slice. Or, if it's Wednesday, a sandwich. There are people who never miss sandwich Wednesday.

But back to the main attraction. The pizza at L'Industrie finds a way to stand out in a very crowded field without getting too crazy. Part of the secret is the way they bake the pies. Massimo points to the oven and tells me they were one of the first places to use an electric oven. There's a lot of talk about coal or wood-burning ovens, but with electric they can play around a little more with how the pizza comes out. They can also experiment with different toppings since they can bake at higher or lower temps and know it'll come out right.

Save room for dessert. L'Industrie is serious about their baked goods and especially their soft serve, which they change up weekly. And if you're in the city but can't make it to Brooklyn, don't worry: They've got another location in the West Village.

TIP

That's how they came up with two of their most famous pizzas: fig jam and bacon, and the burrata pie. Both are so damn good. Eat either and you'll get a sense of how their oven impacts the outcome. There are maybe a thousand places to get pizza in the city, but L'Industrie found that the way to stand out was to be a New York pizza place first, and also to use some old Italian tricks to make sure your customers are happy with what you make.

LUIGI'S PIZZA

686 FIFTH AVENUE

Brooklyn has produced more pizza legends than anywhere else in America, from the late Dom DeMarco of Di Fara to Mark Iacono of Lucali. Whether it's a slice you want or a Neapolitan pie, it's hard to find a place that does it better than the County of Kings. When Lil Mo Mozzarella says Giovanni Lanzo is "the Guy" you go to for pizza, you listen.

Everything about Luigi's is old school. It's been that way since Giovanni's dad, Luigi, opened the shop in 1973. Today his son is proudly carrying on the traditions his immigrant parents taught him as a child. It's the little things, like the green and red sign surrounded by blinking lights to the Coca-Cola menu board right above where Giovanni tosses pizza dough up in the air, and the T-shirts that say "Brooklyn: The greatest country in the world," because Giovanni grew up believing this borough was its own nation. "I was in the fifth or sixth grade and my teacher asked us to write down our favorite country, and I wrote 'Brooklyn,'" he explained to me as he flipped some dough up in the air. "And she

TIP

Pick up a loaf of lard bread from the famous Mazzola Bakery in Carroll Gardens and see if Giovanni will slice it in half and make a pizza out of it for you. "The holy grail of bread," Giovanni says, before adding, "I'm gonna improve it by adding sauce and cheese!"

tells me, 'Giovanni, Brooklyn isn't a country; it's a little piece of New York.' I look at her, and I remember thinking that it's got everything I need. It's the country for me."

Luigi's is as real a deal as it gets. He doesn't mess around with too many crazy toppings. The crust is proofed and prepped so every slice he serves comes out with that perfect balance of crunch and give, and Giovanni is adamant about sourcing the kind of ingredients someone from Italy would appreciate. The real catch is in the sauce. When I was in there with Lil Mo, he looked at Giovanni and said, "You're the only one who uses Sunday sauce on his slice, right? I don't see anybody doing that." I remember Giovanni looked disappointed. "Used to be everybody did it that way," Giovanni

replied, "but now I'm the only one that I know." And he's right: I don't know any places that make a slice with the sort of tomato sauce old nonnas spend hours on.

Italians take their sauce seriously. Pizza sauce is one thing, usually pureed tomatoes with a little seasoning. But Sunday sauce is a whole process that mothers and nonnas would cook for the whole family, made with fresh onions, garlic, maybe some carrots, some seasoning, and usually some meat to beef it up. The whole process is time-consuming. They call it Sunday sauce because it's something the whole family could help make on Sunday. Usually it has meatballs, sausage, braciole, and whatever else is around, but Luigi's version is vegetarian, but when Giovanni serves up a square from the Sicilian pie he puts the sauce on, Lil Mo doesn't mince words after he finishes his piece. "I'm gonna put this in Brooklynese: You don't eat this, you're a momo."

NENES TAQUERIA

14 STARR STREET

ew York City is one of the great food cities in the world, yet finding good Mexican food can sometimes be challenging. Why this is, I have no idea, but Bushwick bucks the trend. Walk around the area long enough and you'll find women selling homemade churros and hole-in-the-wall tamale spots run by people who are starting their American dream. You *can* find great Mexican food; you just have to look. "That's part of the reason I got motivated to do this," Andrés Galindo tells me just before the dinner rush is about to hit his spot and he has to jump back behind the counter.

Since it opened in 2020, Nenes Taqueria has made it a little easier for people who don't want to get on a plane to Mexico City or even Los Angeles to find incredible tacos. Andrés brought Mexico to Brooklyn. His résumé is filled with fine-dining gigs like Ai Fiori and Jean-Georges, but after six months in his family's native country during the pandemic, Andrés came back and saw there were no kitchen jobs available since

> **TIP**
> Go with a group and get a Mexican pizza. It's a lot of food and everybody should experience it.

everything had closed. "What better time to open a business?" he figured. "Our family is a three-generation taco family. My grandfather had a shop that's still there," and Andrés is continuing the legacy, serving the family's take on carnitas. "But we change it up and serve it as birria."

That's what Nenes has become famous for. The rich, tangy meat stew is the center of the small space's universe, available inside empanadas and tacos, but also on dishes with a twist, like one of the most incredible bowls of ramen you'll find in Brooklyn, as well as a Mexican pizza that's out of this world.

Andrés and his family come from Puebla, a part of Mexico he points out is better known for its mole poblano, and not so much for its birria. "It's funny how we got the recipe, since there's no birria cookbook I've seen." They went on Google and YouTube to figure out how to rework his grandfather's recipe. The results have created steady lines out the door. The success is rewarding for Andrés, but what

he's proudest of is that he gets to do it in a neighborhood he's known for years, with his mother by his side.

"We grew up on this street and I went to the middle school up the street. When we first came to the States we lived in the middle of the street, then we moved to the corner, then a few blocks down near Knickerbocker Park." And the spot where he serves tacos today was a place he regularly visited as a kid. "I used to come here when it was a deli. It was a dollar for a piece of fried chicken. I'd stuff myself."

I used to live down the block, and I remember the old bodega that used to exist in the space before Nenes. Andrés has retained that spirit. You can walk in and buy candy, soda, even piñatas from Mexico. As for the dollar fried chicken that used to be there, "Probably not bringing that back," he says with a grin. "But you never know."

PEPPA'S JERK CHICKEN

738 FLATBUSH AVENUE

Shelley Worrell probably knows better than anybody where to get good jerk chicken. After all, she did get the Brooklyn area around Flatbush, Church, Nostrand, and Utica avenues named Little Caribbean.

"Peppa's," she told me without pause when I asked.

Gavin Hussey opened Peppa's in 1995. Growing up in Jamaica as one of twelve kids, Gavin says his job was "the one who'd come home and cook for everybody." He developed a knack for understanding how to balance the flavors you can find all over the island on fish, goat, and vegetables, but especially on chicken. "That's the inspiration," he says.

And at Peppa's, that inspiration falls right off the bone. It's got that kick you want from jerk, but the meat is so juicy and tender that you'd likely pay double for something like it at a restaurant in Manhattan, except it wouldn't be nearly as delicious. You can see why when you

> **TIP**
> Of course get the chicken, but if you like fish, the porgy is excellent, and a little hot sauce brings it to another level.

order, with the cook working over the chicken breasts and legs above an open fire right behind the cashier. Your order comes with the slightest touch of char. Smokey and tangy with the sort of spice that doesn't kill you, but you definitely want an order of rice and beans, maybe some plantains, and probably some fries as well. You also need some mac and cheese. Essentially, everything they make is good, but the chicken is the centerpiece.

Great food is important, but in a place like Brooklyn, especially a neighborhood like Little Caribbean, being connected to Jamaica or other parts of the Caribbean is the secret seasoning you put on your chicken. "[Gavin] does a lot of community events with us," Shelley tells me. One day, you'd see Peppa's at a big, ticketed food event; the next day he'd be doing a community event for free. "We'd take him to the grills in Prospect Park and they give away food to people. Or if the park is having a fundraiser, we'll bring a few businesses from the neighborhood, and Peppa's is always in popular demand."

That's how you become an institution in New York City: being active in your community and being here for a long time. Bad stuff doesn't have a long shelf life here. If something sticks around, it's usually because it's good. Peppa's is a place people know and love whether they're from the West Indies or anywhere else, because it's an anchor for the neighborhood. And yeah, having incredible chicken helps. "People around here love food," Gavin says. He knows he's got to give them the best.

PETER PAN DONUT & PASTRY SHOP

727 MANHATTAN AVENUE

There are certain things you don't have to go far for in New York City. Pizza, coffee, a copy of the *Daily News*, donuts. From Dunkin' to bougie spots, if you want a donut, you're likely not going to have to travel far. But anybody who has spent time in Greenpoint knows there is one place that stands out as *the* donut spot: Peter Pan.

"When this place was opened in 1954 by this Italian couple named Phil and Lucielle, they didn't have a lot of donuts," Demetri Siafakas says. Demetri's family purchased the spot in 1993, and Demetri, his brother, Spyros, and their mother, Donna, are almost always working alongside the servers in their instantly recognizable teal-and-pink outfits.

Go in around the Fourth of July and they have a strawberry glazed with red, white, and blue sprinkles. During the Easter holiday, they've got donuts with Peeps on them, and in February you'll likely spot somebody walking out with a heart-shaped donut for their valentine. Every donut I've had there is delicious, and I've had more than a few. But if he had to guess, Demetri says, "Cream chocolate sprinkle is the Greenpoint donut," favored among locals.

On one visit, I brought my friend benny blanco along. Benny loves to eat, and when he ordered the top-tier egg and cheese, he had them add turkey sausage and make it on a glazed donut. The woman behind the counter was unfazed. She's seen it all. Benny dipped it in ketchup and Cholula hot sauce, took a bite, then shook his head. "Insane" was all he could say.

Peter Pan has served as a meeting place for everyone from politicians to cops, Polish

The bacon, egg, and cheese is one of the best you'll find. You don't have to get it like benny—they serve them on rolls. But if his reaction was any indicator, maybe you *should* get it on a glazed donut.

TIP

can hear what people near them are saying. But that's sort of the beauty of what always made New York diners so perfect. It's a community spot. It's a place where people go because they want to be around other people, to see Demetri and his family, but mostly because they want one of the best donuts in the city.

It's also got a tie to the Marvel Cinematic Universe. The place that sells Greenpointers their honey dip, chocolate cake, blueberry buttermilk, and apple crumb donuts was re-created for *Spider-Man: No Way Home* as the place Zendaya's MJ works part-time.

neighbors, musicians, artists, high school students looking for an egg cream after school, and donut fanatics who will take multiple trains to get there. It's a landmark because it's good, but Demetri says there's another reason: "Diners are universal, and this place feels like a diner." Whether it is or isn't a classic diner is hard to tell. Its counter seats over a dozen people, and everybody is close enough to each other that they

POP'S POPULAR CLOTHING

7 FRANKLIN STREET

Sure, Soho, Madison Avenue, and the Lower East Side are where people flock to when they want to go shopping for Gucci or Supreme, but *everybody* goes to those places, and the prices are crazy. That's one reason to make the trip to Greenpoint and visit Pop's on Franklin.

Steve Rosenberg and his family have been around north Brooklyn in one form or another since 1934. "My grandfather, when he came to this country from Poland, he was carrying wet sacks of laundry, and he decided he needed to do something better.

So he decided to buy some used clothing, then resell it, then buy more and do the same thing."

Eventually, a business started, and Steve's dad, Irving, took over. They began selling used clothing to Brooklyn longshoremen and truck drivers. Steve, who grew up working in the shop, eventually took on a larger role and noticed how their customers seemed to be getting

> **TIP**
>
> Places likes Pop's are becoming rare in NYC, but if you can't make it to Greenpoint to visit Steve's store, I'm also a big fan of Dave's in Manhattan and Frank's Sports Shop in the Bronx.

younger over time. They also didn't look like they did much manual labor. Long before everybody standing in front of you to get coffee was wearing a Carhartt beanie, Pops was the place to go. Today, workwear is trendy. It's definitely been helpful to the business, but with the way trends come and go, Steve always has to stay on the ball. He has to make sure stuff is stocked that will get both creative directors and carpenters in the door.

In 1995, it took some convincing to get Irving to move from his little shop in Williamsburg that the *New York Times* called "gloomy," but his son, Steve, knew they had to expand if things were going to keep going. These days, everything at Pop's is new. You'll see bricklayers browsing next to baristas and graphic designers. And unlike most trendy boutiques, Pop's prices are reasonable. Still, it's never easy for a place like Pop's, but Steve won't argue with the customers who are coming in because he runs the best place to pick up Red Wing and Timberland boots, denim that's made to last, and, of course, beanies. Pop's is workwear heaven.

QUIMBY'S BOOKSTORE

536 METROPOLITAN AVENUE

 illiamsburg has gone through a lot of phases. From working-class neighborhood to bohemian enclave, the area is now one of the most popular and expensive parts of the city. The low rents and big spaces once available to poets and sculptors are all gone, and a lot of the independent businesses have been replaced by the likes of Whole Foods and the Apple Store. That's why Quimby's is such a welcome and important place.

Located a few steps from the Metropolitan Avenue L stop, Quimby's has its roots in Chicago, but it feels more at home in Brooklyn. Steven Svymbersky has

been involved with Quimby's from its start more than three decades ago. He opened the Williamsburg spot because he thought the neighborhood could use a place that specialized in DIY zines, LGBTQIA+, feminist, and BIPOC literature.

"The family who owns this building totally went to bat for me," Svymbersky recalls. "They said they want to turn this stretch of street into the cool part of Williamsburg. It's important to them."

At Quimby's, you can get stuff you can't get anywhere else, like books on the occult and altar candles to decorate your home (or altar) with. Perfectly curated

TIP

Next door to Quimby's is Desert Island Comics, which is the best underground comic and graphic novel shop in the city. If you go to one, go to the other.

poetry chapbooks, zines produced off a copy machine, used paperbacks, and niche magazines are other items you'll find here.

"Every bookstore is my church," Steven says. "They're holy places for me, but it always bothers me when it feels like they just put a bunch of books on the shelves and that's all. They don't think about the vibe. I like it that people come in, maybe they don't know what they're walking into, but they want to be here and not leave."

Even though it started out in another city, Quimby's has the vibe of the sort of place you used to find on the Lower East Side or in the East Village in the 1980s or '90s. It's a bookstore with a punk ethos—for outsiders, by outsiders. In a neighborhood like Williamsburg, which became popular as a place where artists could live and work, Quimby's feels like one of the few places left that is both weird and welcoming at the same time.

SACRED VIBES APOTHECARY

376 ARGYLE ROAD

ew York City is a stressful place, and our lifestyle choices here aren't always the healthiest. This is the city that hosts a hot-dog eating contest on Coney Island every year and has bars on every corner. We need to find some balance, and this cozy shop in Ditmas Park is where people come when they need their dandelion root or rosehips. When you step inside, I swear, your entire mood changes. Jars filled with powders, roots, and herbs line the walls, and it's also one of the best-smelling places in the city. That might sound funny, but one true

NYC stereotype is that there are a lot of questionable odors.

"My mom has been an herbalist basically our entire lives," Lauren Burke-Rincon tells me. Her mother, Karen Rose, has become something of a celebrity among people looking to live a little better. She's a master of botanical medicine who started learning about the healing power of plants growing up in Guyana. When she came to America, Karen continued to study roots and herbs used in traditional medicines from all over the globe. She started out as so many people do, working a corporate job to

You can go to any bodega and find Rhino pills, but if you really need some horny goat weed, Sacred Vibes has the real stuff.

TIP

the shop but also other nearby neighborhoods. Little Caribbean is not too far away, and pockets of communities that include people from Ukraine, Mexico, all over the African continent, the Middle East, and other parts of the world are just a few stops away off the Q train. There are numerous communities nearby that still use herbs in everyday life, but the shop is also in a part of Brooklyn where you get plenty of people who picked up yoga in the last few years or use a meditation app to ground themselves before their Zoom meetings. Karen's timing was perfect. Today, her shop is the go-to of its kind.

Karen and her kids are knowledgeable, warm, and inviting, just like the space. It feels like an oasis from the commotion outside. When I walk into the store, I'm immediately at ease, and I always come away feeling like I learned something and that I want to try a little harder to live a little healthier.

pay the bills. But in her spare time, she was finding clients who wanted to know what herbs could help them feel better. "Then in 2009 she decided it was time to get a space," Lauren says. So the family picked up from Arizona and moved back to the place Karen arrived when she moved to America: Flatbush. "She knew this area would be seeking that stuff."

When she says "area," she's talking not only about the neighborhood around

SETTEPANI BAKERY

602 LORIMER STREET

pened in 1992 by chef Nino Settepani, who immigrated here from Sicily, the bakery with Nino's name feels like the natural border between Williamsburg and Greenpoint on Lorimer Avenue, two of the neighborhoods that have seen the most transformation from working class to big money over the last few decades. That's why being more than simply good has been a must for Nino and his wife Leah Abraham, an Ethiopian Eritrean immigrant who also put in time in the NYC food world up in Harlem. Long before Williamsburg was a place people had no problem schlepping to for a good meal, Settepani was holding it down. It has always been a place people would transfer trains to get to.

The thing I love about Settepani is how unassuming it is. Everything in New York is trying to grab your attention, but Settepani just exists. I've heard of people who live nearby passing it for years until they discover they've been walking by

If you can't make it to Brooklyn, they ship their Nutella panettone nationwide. It makes a perfect gift for the holidays.

T/P

really all you need to have the top of your head blown off, but it's almost impossible not to finish the whole slice. A delicious sin against nature.

But one cannot live on Nutella-filled panettone alone, so I usually save my order for the holidays. Instead, stop in for savory stuff. The tomato focaccia is nuts, and the round loaf of casareccio bread is perfect, especially when having company over. Everything at Settepani's is good, and I don't think we need to wait another sixty or seventy years to say it: The place is a local institution, a Williamsburg landmark that never fails to please.

one of the best bakeries in north Brooklyn. When they finally do walk in, they find a counter filled with homemade cheesecakes and rainbow cookies. But what the bakery is actually most famous for is panettone. And not just any old panettone, but a chocolate panettone filled with Nutella. One bite is

TAQUERIA RAMIREZ

94 FRANKLIN STREET

There's a reason people have been obsessed with Taqueria Ramirez since they first flicked on the open sign in 2021: They make some of the best tacos in New York City, and when a place kills it with tacos, people pay attention. It makes sense, because you can eat them on the go. They're like an egg-and-cheese or a hot dog, the sort of thing you'll see someone chowing down while walking. But owners Giovanni and Tania think you should chill for a few minutes and enjoy your taco at their spot. These tacos come made to order and taste best a minute or two after they're served.

In a city filled with food sitting for hours under heat lamps that you take and go without a single thought, Taqueria Ramirez stands out because there, a guy blowtorches the meat, puts it in a tortilla, and you've got one of the best tacos in the tristate area. With Giovanni and Tania's tacos, you are getting an authentic culinary experience because they're both from

Mexico. You can also see how diverse the food scene is in Mexico: Giovanni hails from Mexico City, and Tania grew up to the north in Coahuila, closer to the Texas border. So there are a lot of different influences mixed into Taqueria Ramirez, and they all come together starting with your first bite.

"I'd been holding on to this big idea to do this for a long time," Giovanni tells me. He and Tania had been working in a photo studio, and in his spare time, Giovanni made tacos for coworkers and hosted a few pop-ups. He said it was a casual thing that came out of "a need for good tacos."

He's underselling it. When you get to the counter at Taqueria Ramirez, you see how seriously they take their tacos. It's a small setup, and you won't get your basic shrimp tacos or some wimpy, underseasoned chicken breast on a tortilla that feels like wet cardboard. Instead, you see a guy with the blowtorch giving the

meat a perfect char like you've probably never had unless you've had tacos from a street vendor in Mexico City. There's a pan called a comal choricero, where they cook the meat. Inside the pan, tripa, or beef intestines, stews in a broth that you might find yourself wanting a cup of on its own. To the left, you've got a beautiful spinning cone of pork for the tacos pastor, and they'll put your choice of meat and toppings on sunny yellow tortillas. And the beauty is that everything is cooked in lard. Every bite is incredible.

"I have to pinch myself every day," Tania tells me as we watch the line that never seems to end. They just wanted to make good tacos, and it seems as though a lot of other people wanted that as well.

> **TIP**
>
> Giovanni says they're trying to encourage customers to try many different items on the menu, and he particularly hopes people don't shy away from the house-made spicy salsa they're really proud of. I say try *all* the tacos if you can. Each one is a winner.

VILLABATE ALBA

7001 18TH AVENUE

Sicily plays an enormous role in the story of New York City. The region's influence is impossible to miss around Mulberry Street in Manhattan or Arthur Avenue in the Bronx. Brooklyn also has connections to the Italian island. That's obvious when you walk down 18th Avenue and catch a glimpse of the Villabate Alba sign. The place was named for the small Sicilian town where Angelo Alaimo and his son, Emanuele, were bakers before moving to the United States. After years of hard work, the father and son eventually opened their own place in 1979.

These days, it's a full-on family affair, Angela Peralta says. She's one of Emanuele's kids, and tells me if an employee is not somehow related to the founders, they've likely been working for them for a long time. On the other side of the counter, you have several generations of customers who have been coming for years because they love recapturing a taste of the old country.

"My grandfather and father started with cookies and pastries, a little more simple," Angela tells me. Her husband, Julio Peralta, came into the fold "and started

doing all these fancy things" like beautiful, multitiered cakes that people come from all over to pick up for birthday parties and weddings.

They probably also just want to be there because it looks incredible. Villabate Alba feels almost like some old-school European department store. Painted with murals on its walls and ceilings, it's like a holy tribute to biscotti and cannoli, butter cookies and Linzer tarts, lemon tarts and ladyfingers.

The Bensonhurst neighborhood the family has been situated in for decades is home to a large community of Italian Americans, many with ties back to the same island Angelo and Emanuele originally came from. Whenever I stop in, I figure I'm one of the few people who didn't grow up nearby. Angela knows almost every customer by name, but once she introduced me to a longtime customer and said, "He schleps out from Great Neck." Another regular comes all the way down from the Upper East Side back to the neighborhood he grew up in. The guy was in a black leather jacket with a Yankees cap pulled down low and a pair of dark sunglasses, and he told me he can't get better biscotti anywhere else, so he makes the weekly journey to Brooklyn for his fix. That's the best way to sum up the vibe at Villabate Alba. People are crazy loyal to it. You'd think that's an easy-enough concept, but it's one you don't see people putting into practice enough these days.

TIP

I brought Rosanna Scotto and Bianca Peters to Villabate Alba for a segment on their *Good Day New York* show. They were huge fans of the cannoli, which is made with ricotta all the way from Sicily. Would highly recommend you get at least one. Rosanna's favorite bakery is Aunt Butchie's, which is a short drive away in Bay Ridge if you want to try some of her favorite pastries.

YESTERDAY'S NEWS ANTIQUES & COLLECTIBLES

428 COURT STREET

People love my friend the Green Lady of Brooklyn because, well, it's hard not to. If you don't like seeing a nice woman who is always dressed head to toe in green, then I'm guessing you're not a fan of Kermit the Frog or Yoda, either. A lot of people don't know that the Green Lady is also an incredible watercolor artist. She has her work hanging throughout her apartment in beautiful antique frames. I asked her where the frames came from, and she told me about Yesterday's News, one of her favorite places in her Carroll Gardens neighborhood.

There are countless people selling old, vintage, odd, and overlooked things from the past, but J.P. and Colleen Ferraioli bring something a little different to the table. First, they're from the neighborhood, and have been selling their wares since 2001. J.P.'s

TIP

They've got furniture and plenty of big items you'll see when you walk in, but check out the bins of black-and-white photos. Between that and all the old matchbooks and buttons, there are loads of little things you'll spend the most time looking through.

obsession with antiques and vintage items goes back to his childhood, when he started collecting Coca-Cola memorabilia. From there, it grew into picking up more old stuff he just thought was classic and cool.

"We don't really focus on any specific decade," he tells me. "We started carrying some stuff from the 1980s, but mostly it's stuff from before then. As long as we like it and think customers will, it fits in the store."

I can't tell you how many times I've been to local flea markets and vintage shops and the prices were fifty times more than what the item probably cost fifty or sixty years ago when it was originally purchased. That's not the case at Yesterday's News. J.P. and Colleen keep prices reasonable, "because that's how we move inventory in and out," he tells me.

And that's how Yesterday's News became a local legend. Students looking to decorate their dorm rooms with something other than Ikea furniture descend into the shop in hopes of finding a cool chair or a vintage picture they can tack on their wall.

Set designers, people buying multimillion-dollar brownstones, and people just looking to spruce up their studio apartment all make the trek to the Carroll Gardens staple. You rarely see the same thing twice. If you sleep on buying that stack of vintage *Playboy* magazines you thought would look cool on your coffee table, they'll be gone next week. That beautiful oak desk where you could write your novel, or the set of jadeite dishes you want for your next dinner party, this is the place to get those kinds of things. J.P. is always on the hunt, and he keeps his sources secret so none of the new-school overchargers can find out where he gets his stuff.

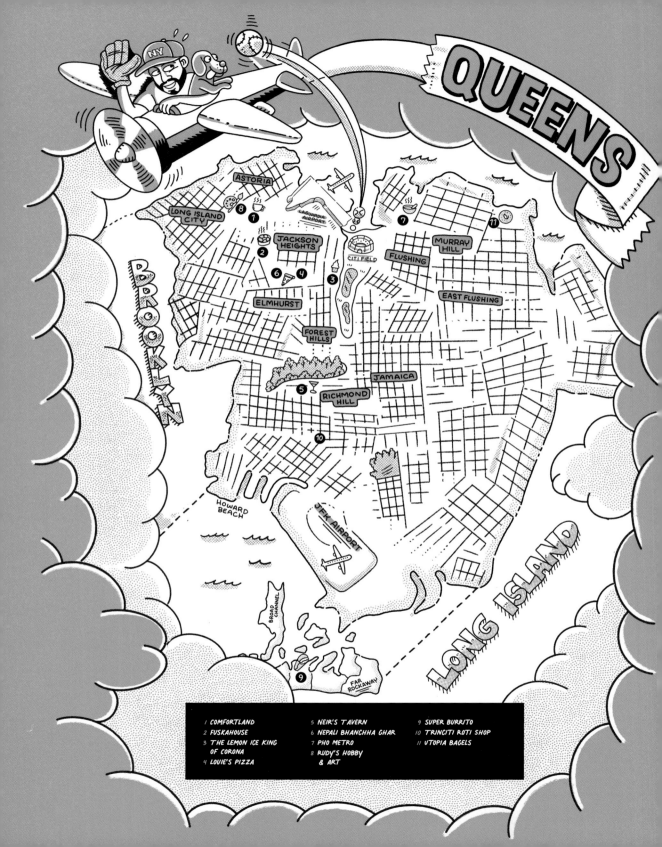

People don't realize how important Queens is. If you've turned on a TV set in the last fifty years, there's a good chance you stopped by Archie Bunker's house in Astoria in the 1970s, or maybe you visited George Costanza's parents in the same neighborhood while watching *Seinfeld*. *The King of Queens* took place in Rego Park, and *Awkwafina Is Nora from Queens*'s title character lives in Forest Hills. But television isn't the only place Queens had an impact. Food, style, music, comic books—you name it. Queens shapes culture.

It makes sense that the huge Unisphere still resides in Flushing Meadows–Corona Park decades after it was created for the 1964 New York World's Fair. While New York is one of the most diverse cities in the world, nowhere else has the variety of Queens. Literally. You can't find another place where as many different languages are spoken, not just in New York or America, but in the whole world. 800 languages! If you spend enough time in Queens, you'll hear Spanish, Urdu, Greek, Tagalog, Yiddish, Nepali—and nearly another 300 other languages spoken along Roosevelt Avenue alone.

Because of that diversity, Queens is where you can get the best in class of whatever you're looking for, from Italian ice to Bengali food. Queens is where Simon & Garfunkel, the Ramones, Run-DMC, Mobb Deep, and Nas all come from. It's where Peter Parker lives in comic books when he's not flying around as Spider-Man, and where Eddie Murphy's Prince Akeem hoped to find his queen in the classic movie *Coming to America*. In recent years, neighborhoods like Long Island City have become some of the most desirable in all of NYC, and Queens has also become a center of the fashion world, with brands like Aimé Leon Dore, Awake, and Kith coming out of there.

Queens is where you go not just to experience New York City culture, but nearly every other culture around the globe.

COMFORTLAND

40—09 30TH AVENUE

I love Comfortland, but I realized I'd never been there with my pal Mike Chau, of @foodbabyny, and his family until now. Seeing how much his kids love it too illustrates how the place is a hit with anybody, regardless of age. But what do you order? Is there a number-one item you shouldn't miss? I once asked this of the server at the front window. "You can't really go wrong," they said. "Like Ray Allen shooting the basketball, we never miss."

While the joke was decent, it made me, as a Knicks fan, a little ashamed that a place in New York City couldn't use a Knicks player as an example of a great NBA shooter. My sadness washed away when James Avatar, the multimedia mastermind as well as weekend window guy, front-of-house manager, and brand ambassador of Comfortland, brought out the Chicken Biscuit Buddy.

"No, man," he said when I repeated the words "chicken biscuit buddy" back to him. "It's the *Chicken Biscuit Buddy*. This is the game changer. This is the new breakfast sandwich everybody needs to eat."

I couldn't argue with that, but I'd say you're getting two meals in one. It's got fried chicken with bacon, egg, and American cheese in the middle, with

"There's nothing like this in Queens," Mike says as his daughters split a Rainbow Cake milkshake, which is exactly what you'd imagine, multicolored sprinkles and all.

If you're an adult, you'll love this place. If you're a kid, you'll love this place. If you're an adult with kids, well, you've got your spot in Queens all picked out. Mike says you can't go wrong with the donuts. As for me, the rainbow cookie crumb cake is an idea on another level, and it's as delicious as it sounds.

TIP

"You know pumpkin spice is so big in the fall, but not everybody likes pumpkin, so we got a sweet potato milkshake and it's the bomb," James says. I take one sip of it, and James was not lying. "We've got fries with truffle oil and white parmesan cheese sprinkled on top. We've got the Freaky Friday, which tastes a lot like a Big Mac . . . except that it's two pieces of fried chicken." He won't tell me how they figured out the secret sauce, but I try not to ask too many questions when something is this good.

chipotle aioli and maple Tabasco sauce syrup poured on top. And yes, it's in a biscuit. Half of it is enough to carry you past lunchtime. That's basically how Comfortland works. It's serious comfort food. The place is fun and weird, and everybody who goes there has a good time, but it's also serious, because they really put a lot of thought into everything on the menu.

QUEENS

FUSKAHOUSE

7301 37TH AVENUE

T here are really two kinds of food carts in NYC. There are the ones that serve staples like hot dogs and pretzels, and then there are the ones that focus on another sort of local cuisine—local to places often thousands of miles away. You can turn any corner and find someone who serves chicken and rice from the Middle East, then go another block and find jerk chicken from Jamaica, next to another cart that has a perfect chicken tamale with your name on it. You could eat from just about anywhere in the world if you walk around the city, but to get a taste of the local Bangladeshi community, you've got to go to Jackson Heights. I asked my friend Naq what he thought I needed to check out and he said one word: "fuska."

Much like the dumpling, fuska is a variation on something nearly every culture has. It's a deep-fried ball of dough not unlike a donut or johnnycake, except this street food, which is popular across the Indian subcontinent, has a more savory thing going on. Instead of sweet cream inside, or sugary frosting on top, it's filled with tamarind chutney, yellow split peas (matar daal), chopped onions, and bits of potato. Then

it's topped off with some egg, red onion, and chilies. There are other variations depending on who's making it, but Naq told me without any hesitation that the best in Jackson Heights was from the bright green Fuskahouse cart.

How is he so sure? "Trust me," he said. "I'm the originator. Me and my friends started selling fuska a few years ago as Jhal NYC, because it's a popular street food in Bangladesh. We're New York kids with ties to there; New Yorkers love street food, so we figured we'd do it."

Naq is sort of a young godfather of fuska. But now he's also busy being a local hero, helping small business owners as his day job, though he still walks along the avenue keeping tabs on the little empire he started. If he says Fuskahouse is the best, then it's the best.

It's definitely worth the trek to Jackson Heights to eat at Fuskahouse. You can't find this treat at many other places in the city. The semolina shells are deep-fried, then filled with potatoes and yellow split peas, and you dip that in tamarind water for this unbelievable mix of flavors in your mouth. They look like little balls with their tops sliced off, which makes for a really interesting presentation compared to other kinds of street food you find around the city.

Mohammad Rahman runs Fuskahouse, but everybody calls him Masud. He opened in January 2019, really the perfect time to test things out. Only die-hards would stop in the middle of a cold winter day to order from a food cart. But it worked. Word spread and Masud became a fixture. "I went to a few food trucks that made this food from my country and I didn't like the food, so I started my own thing," he says. That alone made me appreciate the guy, but the line halfway down the block to eat his fuska also didn't hurt.

Masud and his crew work hard, making and serving food to other immigrants from Bangladesh and everywhere else. You will have to wait in line for everything on the menu, from their namesake dish to the mango chaat or spicy chotpoti made of potatoes and chickpeas. While you wait, you'll hear so many different languages being spoken that the experience of waiting is worth it. You get to soak in the diversity of the city, and then you get a delicious, inexpensive meal you can eat on the sidewalk.

TIP

When you're finished, order some of their tea. They take it very seriously and it perfectly complements the food.

THE LEMON ICE KING OF CORONA

52–02 108TH STREET

New York City has undergone an ice cream renaissance in the last few years. Places like Ample Hills or Van Leeuwen have lines out the door all summer, and my friends swear that vegan ice cream can be as good as regular. The crazier the flavor, the more popular it seems to be. But sometimes you just want old school, something familiar but singular. For that, go to the Lemon Ice King of Corona. Nicola Benfaremo opened the place in 1944, and when his son, Peter, returned from fighting in the second world war, he ran the place. Eventually, Peter handed over the keys to the current owners, Mike Zampino

and Vinnie Barbaccia, both longtime former employees of the Lemon Ice King. They know people come here from all over the city, because no matter what the frozen trends are, there's only one Lemon Ice King.

Corona is one of those quintessential NYC neighborhoods you can spend all day

TIP

Try all the different flavors. The ices are small and dairy-free, so they won't fill you up too much. The lemon is iconic and a must, the pistachio is really good, but the peanut butter is my favorite. And remember: There's no mixing! If you do ask, you'll look like you have no idea what you're doing.

exploring. Back in the day, it was home to jazz legends such as Dizzy Gillespie and Louis Armstrong, whose brick house on 107th Street is a National Historic Landmark and museum. But ask anybody who knows the area, and they'll tell you that all roads lead back to the little Italian ice spot on the corner of 108th Street and 52nd Avenue. Not ice cream and not gelato, Italian ice is one of those things not enough people know how to get right, but when they do, customers get obsessed. It doesn't have any dairy or eggs in it, so technically Lemon Ice King was way ahead of the vegan frozen-treat trend. It's also insanely flavorful. It's big with locals, but it's also famous among German tourists visiting the city. "We're really big with them because of the show," Mike says. The show Mike's talking about, of course, is the 1990s sitcom *The King of Queens*, which features the show's star, Kevin James, dropping an ice in front of the store toward the end of the opening credits.

The shop started with just the lemon and pineapple flavors but eventually added more to the decades-old hand-drawn menu that sits on the counter. Today you can get chocolate, cantaloupe, root beer, rum raisin, and my personal favorite, peanut butter. There are more than forty flavors to pick from, but mind the house rule: No mixing. Mike isn't going to bend this rule for anyone, not even the mayor. There's no secret code or handshake that can get him to mix banana with strawberry. He's just that confident his ice is perfect the way it is.

"I have a running joke with a friend of mine. He says, 'What if my ma's ill and the only thing that can save her is if Mike mixes an ice?' And I say, 'Better make peace with your mother.'"

LOUIE'S PIZZA

81-34 BAXTER AVENUE #1

It's important to have opinions on things like the best Knicks players ever and favorite *Simpsons* quotes, but when it comes to something like pizza, it's not a bad idea to consult a few experts. No two palates are the same. One of my go-to people to text when it comes to food is my pal Mike Chau of @foodbabyny. And since he lives in Queens, he's the first person who comes to mind when I'm searching for new food places there. When I asked him to recommend a slice spot he loves, he didn't hesitate: Louie's Pizza in Elmhurst. If your New Yorker pal can give you such a definitive answer on such a

tough subject, you have to trust them. You also trust owner Louie Suljovic when he tells you what sets him apart from the hundreds of other pizza spots in the city: "I'm not like anybody else. I don't want to be like anybody else. I'm from this neighborhood. I know my customers and what they like. If they don't like something, they'll let me know, and I listen."

Louie's just built differently. He's one of the most intense pizzamakers I've ever met, but also a person who truly cares about his neighborhood. He's legend around his part of Queens thanks to his pizza, but also because, in the spring of 2022, Louie

That's legendary stuff. Enough to make me

If you aren't in the mood for pizza, Mike's kids crushed a bowl of fettuccine bolognese in front of me and gave two thumbs-up each.

TIP

and his pops, Cazim, ran to the aid of a sixty-one-year-old local woman who was being mugged. The mugger stabbed both Louie and his father multiple times, but the Suljovics were able to hold the perp down until the cops came. Louie tried going back to work after the incident but discovered that both he and his dad suffered collapsed lungs. Louie checked himself into Elmhurst Hospital—a place he made sure stayed fed when it was suffering from some of the city's worst COVID-19 rates during the height of the pandemic—and was back to making pizza a week later.

"Absolutely I'd do it again. I wouldn't even think twice. I'm a human," he says.

and any New Yorker want to support guys like Louie and his father. The best part is that my friend Mike is right: Louie's makes an incredible slice. The pepperoni is particularly great, but everybody swears they make the best grandma slice not just in Queens, but in the entire city. For Louie, there's a simple explanation: quality control. "I have a good slice. It's a slice some people eat every day. It's a slice I eat and that I'd feed to my family."

He is adamant about never sacrificing quality for profit. His body, sure, he'd throw that in front of a knife-wielding attacker, but he'd rather close up shop than serve a less-than-stellar pizza. "People are obsessed with money. It's gone when you're dead, so who cares? What you leave behind is your name and your reputation," he says as he boxes up a pie and hands it to a regular.

NEIR'S TAVERN

87–48 78TH STREET

You've probably noticed there aren't any bars in this book. I'm not a big drinker, and there are plenty of books and websites you can read if you want to know about the city's many bars. So why does this one make it into the book? Well, for starters, it's old, quite possibly the oldest in New York City to operate continuously. McSorley's in Manhattan claims it's the oldest, since Queens wasn't technically part of New York City when a bar was first opened on this site in 1829, and you can make what you want of

that. However, Neir's has two things that will always get me to Queens to say hello: one of the best bar burgers anywhere, and a deep connection to one of the greatest movies ever.

"The burger was important to me when I took over. It had to be a great burger, because a place that I try to make as a true community gathering place, it has to have a great burger as a staple and the heart of where we gather. That's the underlying concept," Loycent Gordon tells me. Loycent took over ownership in 2009 and restored the bar to make it a place where locals as well as people from all over could stop in. Loycent hails from Jamaica, but he understands that a burger is a great unifier. Everybody likes a burger. And this particular burger, with its greens, grilled tomatoes, sautéed onions, pepper jack cheese melting over the side of buns made at a bakery a few blocks down the street, and a special house

If you're looking for the spots from *Goodfellas*, there's one right as you walk in the front door and another at the left end of the bar. Watch the movie before you go and you'll know what to look for.

TIP

sauce, is named after what Neir's is best known for.

It's the Goodfella Burger, named so because once you walk in, it's hard not to notice you're standing in the same spot where Liotta, Pesci, De Niro, and the rest of the wise guys from Martin Scorsese's classic appeared in some of the movie's most iconic scenes. It's also got plenty of other history, including appearing in a few other films, and supposedly it's the place where Mae West started her singing career (when there used to be a larger stage).

But Loycent doesn't want Neir's to just live off being a film landmark. He wants to make sure he's providing a place for people to be comfortable, drink a beer (or several), and eat a delicious burger. "Trust me, it's so much easier to go the other way and serve basic bar food," he says, "but I had to hold on to what I thought was important because I bring my family here, I eat here, and I want to be proud of what I'm serving and for it to reflect my values."

It's a funny twist of fate: Loycent is one of the most decent human beings you'll ever meet, and he took over a bar connected to a movie about a bunch of criminals, including

one who rats on all his friends. But Loycent still has had to fight to keep the place in business, dealing with huge rent hikes that almost put him out of business in 2020.

"I want us to reach our 200th anniversary," he says. "I realized I can't be here all day, every day. And I won't always be here. So how will I cement that Neir's Tavern is an important place? And one of the greatest achievements was having the street outside named after us. No matter what happens, at least people will see the street sign and know there was a bar here, and they'll know it was so important that they named the street after it. And the other thing is, we're listed in the Congressional Record, the history book of the United States. People will always know it existed. The future is to figure out how to gather real community support to help us get to the 200th anniversary in 2029."

NEPALI BHANCHHA GHAR

74–15 ROOSEVELT AVENUE

alk into Nepali Bhanchha Ghar and you're among legends, a dynasty. When the annual Momo Crawl takes place, it's almost a lock that the crown will end up at 74–15 Roosevelt Avenue. That's why my friend Naq took me there.

I met Naq at rallies for Commercial Rent Stabilization, a bill that would protect small businesses and nonprofits from predatory rent hikes. He's an activist who works for the nonprofit Chhaya, which helps small businesses, especially those owned and operated by immigrants. Naq helps people deal with things like confusing paperwork and shady landlords. He knows the city like the back of his hand, and this is his neighborhood. He knows what's good.

"To break it down, Jackson Heights is known as Little India, but it's sort of a misnomer," he tells me as we wait for our food to arrive. "A lot of Indian people moved out of here in the eighties and nineties. Now, it's predominantly Bangladeshi and Himalayan, so a lot of people from Nepal and Tibet."

Naq's family is from Bangladesh, but growing up in Queens means you're a citizen of the world. He's been showing up at Nepali Bhanchha Ghar for a long time. He knows that owner and chef Yamuna Shrestha is a culinary master of many things, but especially the sel roti, a sort of Himalayan donut. I watch Yamuna make them as she sits on a crate over a small drum of bubbling oil. She lets the roti cook in the oil, eyeballing them until they're ready, then she pulls them out with a soda bottle that's been modified to scoop and shape them so their holes are uniform. When the roti hit the table, they remind me more of a johnnycake

you might get in a Caribbean neighborhood and less like something you could order at Dunkin'. But also I can't stop thinking about how it's like a large onion ring without any actual onion inside.

As Naq and I chop it up at our table, we're surrounded by locals enjoying food, talking, and laughing. A couple of items arrive, but then the star of the show hits the table: the momos, Nepal's contribution to the global map of dumplings. It's easy to crush a few of these in a single sitting. They're packed tightly, leaving no room for air like you might get in a soup dumpling in Chinatown or a Polish pierogi in Greenpoint. I imagine that's because people trekking through the mountains need all the sustenance they can get, so they need to make sure every bite counts.

As we eat our meal, we're treated to a show. Dinesh Sunar, one of the servers, also happens to be the Guinness World Record holder for "the most blindfolded

standing backward somersaults in one minute": 22. He's also a stuntman. He pulls up two chairs in the middle of the restaurant, goes to the other side, sprints across the floor, then does a flip over the chairs and lands perfectly before going back to work.

That's Queens for you. Nothing like it.

TIP

If you want to check out the Momo Crawl, it usually takes place in September. It's a party definitely worth going to.

QUEENS

PHO METRO

31—16 FARRINGTON STREET

When my friend Jaeki Cho of Righteous Eats tells me something is the real deal, he means it. In this case it's Pho Metro, an unassuming spot in a strip mall in Flushing that makes some of the best pho in New York. Owner Vinh Tran tells me, "The crazy thing is there are so many places in New York that serve Vietnamese food, but I'd say most of them aren't owned by Vietnamese people."

He tells me he can tell by the pho broth, which coats your entire mouth, with hints of lemongrass and pepper, but also has lots and lots of beef. It's heavy-duty stuff. I can't find pho like it anywhere else.

"I randomly stumbled on this spot," Jaeki says. "I went to the Stop & Shop next door to cop something, then saw the sign for Pho Metro and thought it looked like a Chipotle or something. But I walked in because I was craving some pho. I took one sip and was like, 'Yo, there's something *different* about this.'" He was so into it that Jaeki made Pho Metro one of the first spots he highlighted on his Righteous Eats account.

Order a bánh mì and a side of the pho broth with it. Dip it and welcome to sandwich paradise.

TIP

"The other thing is the Vietnamese coffee," Jaeki says. "They use hazelnut, so it mixes with that condensed milk and those really bitter beans, and it's got this crazy texture and taste like nothing else around here."

Vinh's not just serving food, but also something personal from his culture and family. "There are still a lot of war refugees in America," he says. That includes his aunt, who is one of the co-owners and still works in the kitchen chopping up pork and putting shrimp over the grill. "She came over here and worked in a salon, but her dream was to open her restaurant. So she worked, saved up, and opened this up in 2017." Not long after, Vinh wanted to jump in and help out. Eventually, he realized it was all he had ever wanted to do, and he's been making gallons of the best pho in Queens ever since.

"I was born and raised right here in Flushing," Vinh tells me. "And there weren't a lot of Vietnamese people where I grew up, there weren't Vietnamese places for us to go to. This is my place and my aunt's place, but it shows where my family is from and how far we've come."

QUEENS

RUDY'S HOBBY & ART

35–16 30TH AVENUE

If you've ever walked down 30th Avenue in Astoria, then no doubt you've seen Marvin Cochran, owner of Rudy's Hobby & Art. He's one of the nicest guys in Astoria.

"My adopted name is Rudy," he says with a laugh. "In 1942, my in-laws opened an ice cream parlor here called Rudy's Confectionary."

These days, there isn't any chocolate chip or strawberry getting scooped into cones, but the inside of the shop still retains its charm from the days when kids used to come in and order root beer floats. The floor has the original tile work, and looking at the walls, you can see where the counter once was. His in-laws ran the shop for twenty-five years, then Rudy and his wife took it over, running it for another twenty-five. After fifty years of wear and tear, it would have cost an arm and a leg to fix up the old ice cream shop, so Marvin changed the business plan from milkshakes to model cars, because he really likes model cars and toy trains. It was just easier than renovating and starting from scratch. So Rudy's Confectionary transformed into one of the best hobby shops in the city, a place for model-train enthusiasts, puzzle lovers, and people who love putting things together

with their hands. What was once on offer changed, but the name remained.

"There was no sense changing the name after all those years," Marvin says. He also just sort of took on the name himself. If people walk past him and say "Hello, Rudy," he smiles and waves back.

"I started with trains," Marvin says about making the switch in the 1990s. "Back then, train collecting was very big."

Entering Rudy's is like being transported to a bygone era. There's no digital anything in sight; just paintbrushes, boxes with car kits, and the sound of Marvin's AM/FM radio. I spend so much of my time online and on my phone that it's refreshing to just stand there and talk with Marvin.

Rudy's is one of the last hobby shops in the area.

"It's still big, but not as big as it used to be," he says about model trains. But that doesn't mean Marvin has any plans to put up a "closed for good" sign anytime soon, even though he's in his eighties. "I've been here all these years, and my wife has lived here all her life. She cried when we moved from right here to fifteen houses down the block," he says with a laugh as he rings up my purchase of a Ford Woody Wagon model kit.

SUPER BURRITO

190 BEACH 69TH STREET

ven I can admit that if you want a great burrito, San Francisco or Oakland is going to beat NYC nine times out of ten. But Bay Area transplants Eugene Cleghorn and Sam Neely weren't prepared for just how mid most burritos were when they moved east. "This is something we eat a few times a week," Eugene says about his diet on the West Coast. The Super Burrito guys love living in New York City. Maybe the San Fran Giants and Golden State Warriors games are on a little later out here, but besides that, the only thing they thought was missing was a truly great burrito. So they decided to take matters into their own hands.

Stepping into Super Burrito feels like you've left New York City. Rockaway Beach is its own weird little world, but to Eugene and Sam, it feels familiar. "It's almost always ten or fifteen degrees colder here than Manhattan or Brooklyn," Sam tells me. "And in the morning there's that fog that rolls in, and it feels like San Francisco." They ended up in this location sort of by chance. Eugene spent a few years working at nearby Rippers, the famous Rockaway burger spot. "I wanted to pay as little rent as possible while working less, so a friend and I lived on a boat. We navigated the waterways but didn't have any experience. We didn't have charts; we were going off the GPS on

our boat and took a wrong turn. Finally, we lost the motor, and then we ended up on the open ocean until we parked the boat at Breezy Point and lived there," Eugene says. He and Sam started selling burritos to beachgoers in 2017, then opened a brick-and-mortar location in 2020. While many of the businesses close up shop when the beachgoers stop coming in the fall and winter, Super Burrito is open all year.

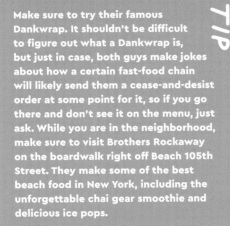

Make sure to try their famous Dankwrap. It shouldn't be difficult to figure out what a Dankwrap is, but just in case, both guys make jokes about how a certain fast-food chain will likely send them a cease-and-desist order at some point for it, so if you go there and don't see it on the menu, just ask. While you are in the neighborhood, make sure to visit Brothers Rockaway on the boardwalk right off Beach 105th Street. They make some of the best beach food in New York, including the unforgettable chai gear smoothie and delicious ice pops.

TIP

They're not trying to rewrite the burrito rule book: They serve a classic, super-stuffed Bay Area beast rolled in some of the freshest tortillas I've had in the city. Eugene points to his tortilla chips: perfect, round, and yellow, almost like the ones you'd get at a ballgame. The cheese dip is made in-house. Eugene and Sam know people want something simple yet excellent. It doesn't need to be that hard, and that's what these two guys from out west understand.

TRINCITI ROTI SHOP

III—03 LEFFERTS BOULEVARD

Many might be surprised to see the line outside of Trinciti in South Ozone Park at nine in the morning. My friend Jaeki Cho of Righteous Eats says it's a normal thing. "Bro, you have no idea," he says. "You ask anybody from around this spot from Trinidad, Jamaica, Guyana, anybody who's West Indian, they'll tell you that this is *the spot*."

The twin island republic of Trinidad and Tobago is the fifth-largest nation in the West Indies, with over a million residents. About half a million people from Trinidad and Tobago live throughout New York City. And many of them live in this section of Queens where Triniciti is located, specifically Indo-Trinidadians who can trace their families back to India. The food is this incredible blend of spices and flavors that might not have all individually originated in the West Indies, but the way they are mixed together is unique to the region. With food from Trinidad, you get a lot of garlic and a type of local cilantro known as chadon beni, but you'll also notice Chinese five spice or cinnamon. And, of course, there's curry. Some dishes may have the same name from one island to the next, but each puts its own spin on them.

Get the Bake and Shark.
Prepare to wait in line.
But the weekend line is
long. Like *really long.*

TIP

Jaeki told me that the Bake and Shark is the must-order menu item. "Bake is literally the bread. It doesn't mean the fish is getting baked." It's a piece of fried bread filled with shark meat, tomatoes or cucumbers, and fresh herbs. "A lot of places in New York try to make this," Jaeki says. "But this is the spot for it. They have the freshest shark. It doesn't have that fishiness. It's clean. Just delicious."

The other thing to get: "Doubles. It's the snack of choice. Two pieces of flatbread with a little tamarind sauce slapped on, and some chickpeas. Nice and easy. When they give it to you it's hot. You never see anybody picking up just one double; you see people popping five of those joints."

"We're here for everybody," Amit Maheepat says of his family's shop. "White, Black, Trinis, Chinese, Jamaican. We're different because some Trini places might be all Indian, but we're not trying to promote one Trinidad alone."

There's a reason that homemade taste is in every bite. You'll notice signs all over the place with specific directions from somebody called Boss Lady. And Boss Lady, Amit's mother, is always watching. She's the ultimate quality control. Signs all over the restaurant tell staff and customers what her expectations are, from making sure the fish doesn't smell funny to making sure not to use too much dough. Amit won't reveal his mother's real name, or even if she's around at that moment, but he smiles and tells me he works like she's always around. That way nothing will slip past her tough standards for making the best Trini food in New York.

UTOPIA BAGELS

1909 UTOPIA PARKWAY

When it comes to debates about the best bagels in the city, Utopia Bagels in Queens is very much in the conversation. They famously make 100,000 bagels a week. And everything is done by hand.

"We've got the Michael Jordan of bagel rolling here," owner Scott Spellman says. Raphy Pérez is the guy he's talking about, and Scott's not exaggerating when he says he's got the G.O.A.T. back there. Raphy has a quarter-century of hand-rolling experience, and Scott claims the guy can roll 1,000 bagels an hour. The number alone is staggering, but what makes Raphy so unique is that he's a throwback. Once upon a time, all bagels were rolled by hand. From the start of the twentieth century into the 1960s, there was even an entire union dedicated to bagel makers in the city, Bagel Bakers Local 338, so to have a guy with twenty-five years of experience behind him means you're eating something made by a master of the craft.

In a way, Raphy is sort of a mascot for the whole idea behind Utopia Bagels. It's all

They are one of the only, if not THE only bagel spot that will make you a GIANT bagel if requested. It's like twenty to thirty pounds. And you can ask them to put anything on it. Great for parties. They also just opened a limited menu location in Midtown.

TIP

the things you might not think about when you're bleary-eyed at eight in the morning and putting in your order, but Scott and his team have thought about every little detail. They don't want to take the easy route for anything they serve customers.

The shared element of every truly great New York City place is soul. You either have it or you don't. The places that don't have it tend not to last, and people are certainly not going to make a trek there the way they would for a spot like Utopia Bagels. What Scott and his crew do is the same thing all the places in this book do: They take pride in their jobs, and the end result is always something better than you can get anywhere else. Is this the best bagel in Queens? Who am I to argue if somebody says that's a fact? I come here all the way from Brooklyn for a bagel.

QUEENS

THE BRONX

WOODLAWN

RIVERDALE 9

VAN CORTLANDT PARK

8

BEDFORD PARK

WILLIAMSBRIDGE

N.Y. BOTANICAL GARDEN

1 12

11 2

BRONX ZOO

MORRIS PARK

5

CITY ISLAND

6

7

"IO"

YANKEE STADIUM

EAST TREMONT

13

10

THROG'S NECK

4

MOTT HAVEN

HUNTS POINT

3

CLASON POINT

EAST RIVER

MANHATTAN

1 188 CUCHIFRITOS	5 CONTI'S PASTRY SHOPPE	8 LIEBMAN'S DELI	11 MIKE'S DELI
2 AJO Y OREGANO	6 DAN'S PARENTS' HOUSE	9 LLOYD'S CARROT CAKE	12 TAKOUT
3 BRONX NATIVE	7 JOHNNY'S REEF	10 LOUIE & ERNIE'S PIZZA	13 THIRD EYE THROWBACKS
4 CASA AMADEO			

Everything you thought you knew about the Bronx was probably wrong. A quarter of it is open space, with some of the nicest public parks in New York City. It also has the fourth-largest Hispanic population in America, so when you hear somebody speaking Spanish, their roots could go back to Puerto Rico, Mexico, the Dominican Republic, or any number of spots from Central and South America. It's got a large Jamaican community that counts the legendary DJ Kool Herc among its ranks, so you can thank him for helping make hip-hop one of the great American art forms. Then there's the incredible Italian American community along Arthur Avenue. Sure, Manhattan's Little Italy is known around the world, but the Bronx's own section has its own style that everybody should experience. On top of all that, my New York Yankees play there.

The old stereotype of the Bronx as a dilapidated wasteland unjustly shapes the way outsiders view it. But once you spend a little time there, you notice all sorts of things, like how incredible the landscape is. One minute you're looking at concrete and old buildings, the next, you realize you're on a cliff and that the Bronx was once a pastoral wonderland. There are gems throughout, from the Hall of Fame for Great Americans at Bronx Community College to the famous zoo named after the borough, and The Bronx Museum.

But it's still the BX, and it will always be the place where the city gets so much of its attitude and style from.

188 CUCHIFRITOS

158 EAST 188TH STREET

ew York has the largest population of Puerto Ricans outside of the Caribbean island itself. So any eatery that calls itself Cuchifritos better be really, *really* good.

Jose Coto is an expert in making cuchifritos, or fried pig parts, which is a delicacy in Puerto Rico and certain parts of NYC. He's been doing it since 1983, so you could say he's the cuchifritos master. "A lot of boxers used to come in here after they trained up the street," he says. The signed pictures and gloves of some all-time greats make up part of the decorations of the popular food spot, but it's the signage that takes center stage. There's the big one out front, with its red, white, and blue bulbs, and then there are the countless hand-drawn ones all over the wall behind the counter telling customers what they can order. Some of the signs were drawn by former employees and are as old as the shop itself.

Just the look of the place should be enough to make anyone want to make the trek up to Fordham Heights, but it's the pork that really gets people traveling. Anthony Bourdain did. That's usually enough

Jose Jr. told me they sell around 300 to 400 rotisserie chickens a day. Just as he told me this, a customer walked up and said, "Best in the city." The most popular item on the menu, though, is the mofongo.

TIP

cost $50, not a few bucks like it is up on 116th. And to wash it all down, 188 Cuchifritos has over a dozen tropical juices they can pour for you.

188 Cuchifritos has been around for over forty years, which is basically almost a century in New York restaurant years. In that time, countless food trends have come and gone, from small-plate tasting menus to chefs creating all kinds of cuisine fusions. But 188 Cuchifritos has stuck to what they do best, and that thing is pork. While not everybody eats pork, those who do know there are people who know how to make it better than anybody else. And like I said, Jose is a master.

of an indication that a place is good, and 188 Cuchifritos lives up to the hype. It's a temple to slow-cooked and deep-fried pork; you can get a plate with some blood sausage and chicharrónes. Or possibly some cuajito, the meaty part of a pig's stomach. It might sound like one of those things that some people might pass up, but if you were in a fancy restaurant downtown, it would

THE BRONX

177

AJO Y OREGANO

621 CRESCENT AVENUE

The Bronx is filled with surprises. You won't come close to scratching the surface with just a single visit. The area's Italian section is the perfect example of this, because you might think it's just about places like Mike's Deli or red sauce, and then you find out the Perez boys at Ajo y Oregano are cooking some of the best Dominican food in the city.

"I get people coming right from the airport from the DR to us," Freddy Perez tells me as a big plate of moro (rice and beans they're especially proud of) is set in front of

us, followed by pots of chicken stew, some pork ribs, and guandules con coco, pigeon peas in a mix of mashed pumpkin and coconut milk that has a beautiful sweet and sour balance. "People are always telling us we're the best Dominican food in the city, and we believe we're number one."

I don't think he's being cocky. It's around two o'clock on a weekday afternoon when I visit, and the place is packed. The space is designed to read as a colorful dining room you'd find in a small Dominican home. People speak in Spanish, Creole, some Albanian and

TIP

This is a Dominican place, so the rice and beans are a must, but don't sleep on the mofongo. I'd say Ajo y Oregano and Cuchifritos are the two places you gotta go for mofongo. Those fried green plantains are not *technically* a New York City dish, but the way people from the DR or Puerto Rico have played such an important part in the growth of the city, I'd say it's just like a knish or bagel that another culture brought with them when they came to New York that has since become ubiquitous.

Russian, and a little bit of Bronx English. Alex Rodriguez could show up and feel at home here, since he grew up down the street in Washington Heights, raised by Dominican immigrant parents long before he put on the Yankees pinstripes. So would other Bronx greats, like Fat Joe or Chazz Palminteri. The reason is simple: The food is excellent and the company is great. But also because Ajo y Oregano take their rum very seriously and will likely offer you a shot. They are from the Caribbean, after all. Even though I'm not a big drinker, I can't say no.

"We want everybody to feel at home here," youngest brother Jeudy Perez tells me. "If you're from the Dominican Republic, great. You'll love our food. If you're from the Bronx, we'll make sure you love our food. We want everybody to come here and enjoy themselves and have a good time."

And most important, they also want you to leave stuffed. The portions aren't small. The family behind this newer Bronx legend (they opened in 2017) want to make sure you don't forget where the best Dominican food is in New York City.

THE BRONX

BRONX NATIVE

127 LINCOLN AVENUE

My friend Amaurys Grullon isn't hard to find when you roll up to Bronx Native. He's the one in the trademark big sunglasses, usually sitting outside on a bench talking with one of his neighbors, greeting people with a loud "Welcome to the Bronx!" And he'll usually throw in a "Yeerrrr" for good measure. Even though he isn't quite sure how that became a thing in his part of town, he knows just about everything else about the Bronx.

Bronx Native, which Amaurys cofounded with his sister Roselyn in 2017, is an ongoing project that shines a light on the Bronx, one of the most special and misunderstood parts of the city. Part gallery, part community space, and part shop, this is a place you can buy shirts or hats designed by Amaurys and other locals while also learning about the past, present, and future of the Bronx. You'll see memorabilia, graffiti, and artifacts from the last few decades, but you also can experience art and have conversations with those who are helping to make people appreciate the most underappreciated part of the city.

"That's AOC's right there," Amaurys says as he points to Representative Alexandria Ocasio-Cortez's signature on the

If you're looking to try a chopped cheese in the Bronx, which is like meeting Mickey Mouse at Disney World, ask Amaurys where to go. He's got plenty of suggestions. Also be sure to visit his favorite cafe, Boogie Down Grind at 868 Hunts Point Avenue.

TIP

wall. "People are already tagging over it, but that's the culture."

All over the store are tributes to people from the borough. Fat Joe, of course. Chazz Palminteri's face can be seen a few times. There's even a Timberland boot with KRS-One's autograph on it. "He was in here and some girl took off her Timb and had him sign it. So we put it up," says Amaurys.

Among the bottles of Arizona iced tea, small plastic barrels of Little Hug fruit-flavored drinks, and cans of Vienna sausages—things you'll find in any good Bronx bodega—there's something more important here, something you can't buy. "We've got a lot of pride here," Amaurys says. "People in the Bronx work. It's a lot of people that come here and this is the first place they know in America. This is where the foundation has been laid for generations of people from all over."

It's hard to find a population of people who grind like people do in the Bronx. And Amaurys, whose family came here from the Dominican Republic before he was born, is the embodiment of that. He's always got a smile on his face, and he's always ready to tell people what's so great about the place where he was born and raised.

Amaurys is always busy, whether he's filming videos of other Bronx natives talking about what sets their home apart or setting up food drives. And in 2022, his big triumph came when he helped create the first annual Bronx Native Day, which was designated by the borough president as October 2 every year.

"That's just how we do it in the BX," Amaurys tells me when I mention how crazy it is that he's able to do so much. "We don't stop."

CASA AMADEO

786 PROSPECT AVENUE

hether it's Tin Pan Alley, CBGB, or the golden age of rap, there is something about New York City that has kept it a center of emerging music. As the Latino community grew during the first half of the twentieth century, people from Cuba, Puerto Rico, and all over the Caribbean brought their sounds and added something new into the mix. As a response, record labels and stores that put out music like salsa and boogaloo popped up to capture and distribute those sounds. Casa Amadeo is a store, but it's also a living, breathing tribute to that era. Its owner,

Miguel Angel "Mike" Amadeo, has not only seen and heard it all, but he's also been a part of it his entire life. That's why the street sign outside the store has his name on it. If you're searching for the oldest Latino record store in the city, look for the corner of Logwood and Prospect avenues and you'll find a sign with Mike's name on it: Miguel Angel "Mike" Amadeo Way.

Born in Puerto Rico, Mike's father came to the States and played music with people like Desi Arnaz just as the American public was starting to catch on to how incredible sounds from the Caribbean islands are.

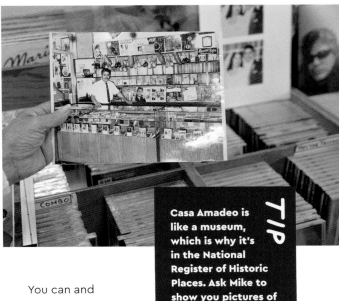

TIP

Casa Amadeo is like a museum, which is why it's in the National Register of Historic Places. Ask Mike to show you pictures of his early days and of his family.

Mike entered the family business, both as a musician as well as an employee at Alegre Records. In 1969, the store known as Casa Hernández, which had opened in another location in 1927, was for sale. Mike took a chance. He was established in the scene, with his own recordings as well as song credits for Latin luminaries like the Queen of Salsa, Celia Cruz. How established? Mike likes to bring up Puerto Rican songwriter José Feliciano, famous for his 1970 Christmas hit "Feliz Navidad," and very matter-of-factly drops, "People talk about Feliciano, 'He wrote this song.' One song," he says putting his index finger in the air. "I got about *250 songs*." After he said this, he started clapping his hands and singing one of Feliciano's compositions.

You can and should buy stuff at Casa Amadeo. Mike's got records stretching over the entire history of Latin music of the last century, but he's also the guy you go to if you want a new acoustic guitar or a set of bongos. Mike has dedicated his life not just to his music, but to his neighborhood and culture as well. "This place was empty once, when the Bronx was burning in the 1970s. Everybody took off. I was the only person here for over a year." I ask him why he stayed put. He tells me he doesn't know, but then he thinks about it for a second. "Everybody walks out of here with a smile on their face. I guess I've got something special."

CONTI'S PASTRY SHOPPE

786 MORRIS PARK AVENUE

In 2021, Conti's, one of the most venerable bakeries not just in the Bronx, but in the entire city, celebrated its 100th anniversary. Its owners don't plan on slowing down. Just don't go looking for Mr. Conti. Ask for Safet Paljevic, who took it over in 2003 with business partner Christina DiRusso and his sister, Senada Paljevic. My friend Anthony MSG introduced me to Saf a couple of years ago after trying to get me to stop by for some time. I am so glad he did, because Conti's is the truth.

"Augustino Conti came over from Italy. He worked at another bakery, and like every immigrant, he wanted to do better. So he purchased this building in 1921 and built his dream bakery," Safet explains as we sit in the expansion to the original store. It's more modern, enough to handle all the orders the bakery gets these days. But the original part of the bakery that the public gets to see, with its tin ceiling, terrazzo floors, and a soda fountain that's been there since 1928, is like walking through a time warp. "It just sort of fell into my lap," Safet says. He grew

TIP

Hit it up on the weekends when they have their killer walnut raisin buns.

up in the neighborhood and knew the guys who bought the place from the Conti family in 2001. Those guys had a falling out and couldn't operate the business. Safet heard how the iconic local spot was in trouble and reached out to the wife of one of the co-owners about stepping in. Today, that former co-owner is Safet's baker.

At Conti's you can get plenty of Italian specialties, but the real draw is the Boston cream pie. It's like eating a cloud made of chocolate and cream. The pie has been in the arsenal for decades. People knew it. So when Safet and his partners took over, they needed to figure out something new to define the bakery for the next century.

Today, custom cakes are a huge part of their business, and the stuff they're making is next level. When I show up, a giant Mets batting helmet cake is getting its finishing touches. Look at the website, and you can see some of their other fantastical creations, from Pennywise the Clown to a cake that looks like a steak. All the while, everything you can pick up from the original bakery is still top-notch. After a century, Conti's has only gotten better.

DAN'S PARENTS' HOUSE

239 CITY ISLAND AVENUE

The best way to describe Dan's Parents' House is that it's like walking into a nineteenth-century home that is actually a time warp to your favorite childhood memories. That's what the husband-and-wife team of Dan Treiber and Reina Mia Brill are going for. I make the trip as often as possible since I like seeing them, but also because I'm always on the lookout for a new *Simpsons* action figure like the one I had when I was ten, a scorecard from a Yankees game from their late 1990s championship days, or some other random piece of ephemera from the last century.

"My childhood home was three blocks from this building," Dan says. "Reina and I bought the house. Which we couldn't afford, so we started Dan's Parents' House as a joke, selling stuff from the attic at the Brooklyn Flea." It wasn't supposed to be a living—Dan ran an indie record label and Reina was a working artist—but as Dan says, "It was the most successful joke we've ever had."

TIP

Reina says you can't leave without buying one of the mystery bags. They cost around $6, come in old paper popcorn wrapping, and you never know what you'll get.

Things were going so well that the couple considered next steps. "In 2016, this building we're in now was going to be knocked down for condos, so we used all of our money and bought this place."

As if the treasures you can bring home aren't enough, seeing the building itself, its old tin ceilings, original wooden beams, and strange twists and turns that lead from one room to another, is worth the ride out to City Island. You get to stand in the middle of local history. "From the 1860s until about 1910, it was Springer's Market, a meat market. From 1910 to 1960, it was J & J Propellers. They made propellers for World Cup boats and built them across the street. And then it was a nautical junk shop called Trader John's from 1960 until we moved in. That place was a beautiful mess."

Today it's less messy but still beautifully chaotic. You never know what you're going to find when you walk in, besides a nice conversation with Dan and Reina. One thing is for sure, you're definitely going to feel like a kid again in there. That's the whole

point. Dan points to the front of the building and mentions there's a spot that over time has eroded into a slope on the sidewalk, allowing puddles to form when it rains. "Every kid has to jump in the puddles, and I've seen a few adults do it also."

Everybody has fun when they go to Dan's Parents' House.

JOHNNY'S REEF

2 CITY ISLAND AVENUE

There's something calming about being at Johnny's Reef. Maybe it's because it's at the end of City Island, so it feels like you're a hundred miles away from New York even though you can see parts of the city as you eat a lobster roll.

"A lot of things look exactly the same as when my family bought it," Sofia Karikas, part-owner and manager, says as I dip some fried scallops in tartar sauce. "They bought it over forty years ago, and it had already been around for twenty or thirty years." She isn't exactly sure when the beloved seafood shack first opened, or when her family took it over, but offers a bit of family

lore. Her dad and his brother decided to go in on Johnny's, and it just so happened that Sofia's uncle was already named Johnny, so there truly wasn't anything that needed to change.

A day trip to City Island, whether it's by car, boat, bike, or MTA Bronx Bx29 bus, is a guaranteed great time. While there's no shortage of seafood to be had along the stretch, to me, Johnny's offers something a little more. The view, meanwhile, never changes. The way the little island is situated along the western end of Long Island Sound, just south of Pelham Bay and east of Eastchester Bay, provides a look at parts

TIP

Bring a crew and order to share. The fried shrimp is great, and the calamari is hard to pass up. But don't sleep on the steamed section. The scallops are a winner there. You will also want to make a day of checking out the rest of City Island. It really is one of NYC's best-kept secrets.

have the means to get around and you're going to end up somewhere on a whim, consider coming here. Looking out at the water while eating fried seafood at Johnny's Reef is my idea of doing New York City right. Order the fried shrimp, fried porgy, or fried lobster tail, maybe some fried chicken wings, and if you're feeling fancy, they've even got fried frog legs. Some of my friends swear by the Henny colada—which is exactly what it sounds like. It's a piña colada made with Hennessy cognac. Have one of those, and all that fried food, and you should be pretty good for the rest of the day.

of the city (and even Long Island) that few vantage points give you. It's not hard to imagine somebody two or three hundred years ago standing in the same spot looking out and wondering what the future holds.

Today, City Island is one of the more overlooked parts of New York, partially because it isn't easy to get to. But if you

LIEBMAN'S DELI

552 WEST 235TH STREET

Liebman's is the only kosher deli in the Bronx, and it's a deli in the truest sense of the word. On any given day you'll see locals just sitting and talking at Liebman's. They really don't make 'em like this anymore.

"My dad didn't have much knowledge of the food world when he bought this place," owner Yuval Dekel admits. His family came over from Israel, where New York City deli culture isn't as big a deal as it is in other places where New Yorkers have moved, such as Miami or Los Angeles. But Yuval was interested in it and paid attention. Between playing drums in a hardcore band and working early shifts serving food, he figured it was going to be one thing or the other, and the deli won out.

"There's an appreciation for what this place does now. And now it's my place, not my dad's. It allows me more confidence in what we do. I see the sort of newer hipster places in Brooklyn or Manhattan doing deli food, and I used to think what we were doing was kind of corny, but the truth is that

we aren't. We have what people seek. This isn't fake."

Established in 1953, Liebman's is the real deal when it comes to the Jewish deli experience. Liebman's is smaller in size and off the beaten path (unless you happen to be in Riverdale). But that's exactly what makes it worth the journey. This is what they mean by a Jewish New York delicatessen. The house turkey rivals the pastrami they make, and the appetizers they offer, from gefilte fish to stuffed derma (also known as kishka, or stuffed beef casings). The coffee is hot and the cans of Dr. Brown's are cold, but the best part is the atmosphere is chill. You can sit there for hours.

LLOYD'S CARROT CAKE

6087 BROADWAY

People say Lloyd's makes the best carrot cake in the world. Once, when I brought one of their cakes to a friend's birthday party, I got to see the magic in action. Coincidentally, somebody else brought a carrot cake from another place that shall remain nameless. We taste tested the two, and the unanimous winner was Lloyd's.

Brandon Adams grew up hearing stories like that, but he knows in the end that the cake his late father, the namesake of the store, debuted in 1986, is the best of the best.

"My father came from St. Thomas. He had a recipe from his grandmother that he brought with him to the States when he came here to play basketball."

TIP

There's another Lloyd's in Harlem, but if you make it to the one in the Bronx and it's a nice day, grab a piece of cake and sit across the street at Van Cortlandt Park. It's one of the city's best public spaces.

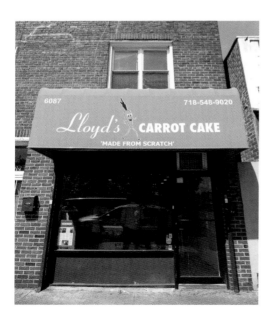

Lloyd Adams was drafted in 1972 by the Washington Bullets. He had his eyes set on a pro career, but an injury derailed his hopes. He stayed in New York. "Back in the day, he was the only person he knew with cable, so he'd have friends over to watch the Knicks. He'd make some carrot cake and they'd watch the game. After a while, friends started telling him he should sell it because it was so good. So he started a wholesale business."

It wasn't until Lloyd dropped off a sample of his carrot cake at the legendary Sylvia's that things started to change. The Harlem restaurant immediately put in orders. Word got around, and people started making their way up to Harlem to get a cake for their dinner parties.

"The product speaks for itself," Brandon says. "Once people taste it, they're hooked. It's very polarizing. You're either with it or you're not." He points out that his family version is different than others you might find. It's moist and not overly sweet. "It's

built this cult following. People try it and they get hooked."

After Lloyd passed away in 2007, his wife, Betty Campbell-Adams, took over the operation. The company continued to grow until Betty's passing in 2020. Today, Brandon and his sister Lilka are keeping the family's legacy alive. Baking, boxing, bagging, whatever they have to do during the day to make sure carrot cake lovers everywhere can get their carrot cake.

"On a week like this, more on the normal side, I'd say we go through eight bags of carrots, so about four hundred pounds. Around Thanksgiving, it's more like a thousand pounds."

And what's beautiful to Brandon is a lot of those orders are from customers who have been buying from Lloyd's for decades. Every year, the place his father built adds more die-hards to the list of people who know where to get the best carrot cake anywhere.

LOUIE & ERNIE'S PIZZA

1300 CROSBY AVENUE

Patsy Ottuso had tried opening pizza spots in New York City and Florida in the 1950s, but it wasn't until 1959, when he opened a shop in the Bronx named after his sons, Louie and Ernie, that things started working. The guys the place was named after eventually took over for their dad. Then, a few decades later, another pair of brothers, Cosimo and John Tiso, took it over. Somewhere in between those two sets of sibling owners, Louie & Ernie's became a Bronx staple. So much so that it's the place my pal Claw, the graffiti legend, suggests when I ask her where to get a good slice in her neck of the woods.

"The Bronx is in a pizza crisis," she tells me as we wait for our slices to come out of the oven. "During the pandemic, a lot of good places closed, a lot of things shifted, cheap pizza places opened up. But this place is *the* place."

My friend Claw has been living in the Bronx for twenty years, and her husband is Bronx born and raised. She says that even when there were more pizza selections around her neighborhood, she'd still make the trip to Louie & Ernie's because it's the real deal. It changed hands from the namesake brothers but went to a couple of guys who know the shop better than

anybody. And since the 1980s, they've been in charge, making sure the place stays the same. Which is to say, perfect.

Louie & Ernie's is a slice and calzone shop, plain and simple. That's what they do. No Neapolitan, New Haven, or Chicago style. They aren't precious about anything. Instead, they have an obsession with consistency, making sure people who ate there in 1989 could walk in today and have the same slice they had back then. But even if a pizza fanatic showed up without any knowledge of the history of the place, in one bite they'd rank Louie & Ernie's among the best pizza spots in the city.

"People come here in generations. I know people from when I started who have dentures now. And I know everybody takes pride in what they do, but being here on a regular basis makes it a little more important. People know me and my brother," Cosimo says as I take my first bite

of a plain slice. It's the perfect amount of cheese melted into tangy sauce, and tastes like what I think of when somebody asks me what, exactly, is New York City pizza.

Cosimo tells everybody to try the plain slice, but the signature dish, he says, is the sausage pie. The sausages actually look like *sausages* and not sad little clumps of meat, and they basically cover most of the slice.

TIP

MIKE'S DELI

2344 ARTHUR AVENUE

hen you walk up Arthur Avenue in the Bronx, you hear a very specific kind of accent. It's that old Italian American New Yawk accent you used to hear parodied in cartoons and spoken by gangsters in movies. You know what I'm talking about: Just listen to local legend Chazz Palminteri speak and you get the picture. When you spend time on Arthur Avenue, you're in a central location for that culture and dialect. Bronx Italian American is very much its own thing, the same way Little Italy and Williamsburg have their own specific flavors.

The Arthur Avenue Market has been around since 1940 and is the true heart of the avenue. Walk in and you can get fresh veggies, pasta they roll right in front of you, steaks, and anything else your nonna would appreciate you eating. But in the middle of it all, you'll find David Greco holding court, handing out slices of soppressata and fresh mozz as he builds some of the most beautiful sandwiches in the city.

"I'm a professional eater, I love to eat, and I take this very seriously," he says while slicing into the house-made focaccia for a Big Mike Combo. It's got ham, mortadella, salami, soppressata, and provolone, but it's not overdone. It's beautiful the way he delicately stacks the meats.

David's family has been in the business for a long time. His dad, and the store's

TIP

Two words: Italian sushi. David is very proud of his genius low-carb idea to layer prosciutto with arugula, mozz, sundried peppers, some fresh basil, a couple turns of the pepper grinder, super Tuscan extra virgin olive oil, and some balsamic. Then he rolls it up with the prosciutto acting as the nori, and what you get is exactly as advertised. It's *Jiro Dreams of Sushi* meets the Bronx.

namesake, Mike, came over from Calabria, Italy, with his twin brother in 1947 and found work at a grocery store on Arthur Avenue. In 1951, he married the boss's only daughter, Antoinetta. David points to a photo on the wall next to where we sit down to eat. "That's my parents. Her brothers were upset because she was standing so close to him," he says of his overprotective uncles.

The couple struck out on their own, and Mike's flair, work ethic, and ties to the old country made him a legend along the strip. Everybody knew Mike and people loved his food. "I learned it all from him," David admits.

The Arthur Avenue Market and Mike's makes a perfect day trip. You can do your shopping, then get a plate of Mike's Italian nachos featuring truffle-flavored chips loaded with red peppers, prosciutto di Parma, fresh basil, parmesan ("the *real stuff*," he says as he grates a generous amount on top), then some balsamic glaze, and a generous couple of tosses before it hits your plate. Everything Mike makes is insanely big. Chances are you'll have leftovers. But if you can actually finish the whole thing, the market is a perfect place to just sit around and relax, maybe talk to some locals, and hear stories of how the street used to be and how it has changed. If you're lucky, David will take off his apron for a few minutes and talk to you.

"I'm not the Godfather of Arthur Avenue," he tells me as he brings out another sandwich to try. "But I've been doing this for over forty years, and nobody does what I do."

He's right.

TAKOUT

2435 GRAND CONCOURSE

The best stuff in New York flows down from the top. The further up you go in NYC, the closer you are to understanding where so much of the culture comes from. Harlem and Inwood in Manhattan and, of course, the Bronx. My friend Claw knows better than anybody. She's been on the scene for a few decades, gaining notoriety first for her graffiti art and then in fashion, bringing street style to brands like Calvin Klein and Vans. If she tells me a spot is hot, I know it's going to be good. And Takout is the sort of place any streetwear person or sneakerhead needs to check out.

Sam Park is the brand manager. He's a local guy who remembers back when guys from the neighborhood were fiending for Pelle Pelle jackets, Polo, North Face, and Timberlands. "A lot of that influence from the nineties, when Bronx graffiti writers started hanging downtown, they were bringing that vibe to a bigger audience." Just like the way guys from the outer boroughs like Jean-Michel Basquiat, Fab 5 Freddy, and Phase 2 did in the late 1970s and early '80s. Sam tells me a big part of the influence is "styles melding," and says the Bronx obviously has its own flavor, but when it meets up downtown and bumps into

Brooklyn or Queens, magic happens. That's sort of NYC style in a nutshell, and Takout is a tribute to that.

"We try to keep it diverse. We've got Jordans and Timbs," Sam says as he points to two of the most iconic footwear brands you're likely to spot in the city. "But we've also got Kuon from Tokyo, Pasadena Leisure Club, New Balance, Taschen books . . ."

People line up almost daily for the limited drops. That's why the shop

has become an important part of the community. Many of the people lining up are from the neighborhood—they come in, get their sneakers, then hang. Sam points outside to Fordham Road. "We're close to so many institutions, from Fordham College to the Bronx Zoo. And not only do we serve the Bronx community, but you've got people coming in and out from Westchester and even Manhattan. Fordham has always been the spot to pick up a mixtape or buy sneakers. Locals, but also kids from Scarsdale or parts of Connecticut, because this was the closest place for them to go. The neighborhood has changed a lot, but it also feels frozen in time because it didn't develop at the same pace as Brooklyn or Queens," Sam says. It's that lack of big

buildings and chain stores that has helped the area retain its soul, and why people still make the journey to cop whatever from Takout. As for me, I swore I wasn't buying anything, but I still walked out with a Yankees fitted, a pair of Nike VaporMax, and another pair of New Balance sneakers to add to my collection.

THIRD EYE THROWBACKS

3004 MIDDLETOWN ROAD

hird Eye opened in November 2019. The idea wasn't to open a traditional vintage store, but more to offer a look inside owner Justin Lebowitz's mind. "When I was younger, I wanted to open a skate shop," he says. He went on to describe one particular skateboard place he used to go to that had a couch where local skaters went just to hang. "I always wanted to make a place like that. Almost like a social club-ish place, but you're able to purchase into it. I used

to make a lot of art before this, but I sort of stopped, so now this is my art, curating this."

If you're a millennial who grew up loving sports and video games, imagine your dream bedroom when you were twelve or thirteen—what would it have? Old nWo T-shirts? Super Mario toys? New York Giants pennants? Pogs? Justin's got binders filled with those. It's a wild assortment of great stuff, all in great shape. He's got old Hawaiian shirts, baseball jerseys from

the 1980s, and old merch from the 2000 Yankees–Mets subway series. A lot of items are for sale, but many are part of the living art installation that is Third Eye Throwbacks. I ask about the VHS tapes behind him, old copies of *Terminator 2* and Spike Lee flicks, *Home Alone* and gritty cop dramas: What's the deal with those? Why aren't they for sale? "People get ticked about it," Justin replies. "They're always asking how I'll show off the collection, but I won't sell anything, but I just want to share."

That's what really makes Third Eye so unique. It's a store, but it's almost like an accidental reliquary of cool stuff we may have forgotten about or lost over time. Justin is a collector and dispenser of memories. "Everything has a price," he says with a grin, before adding, "but for the most part, not really. The closer it is to me, the less of a chance I'll sell it."

TIP

You're a few minutes from all sorts of great Bronx food spots like Empire Bagels and Zeppieri & Sons (people rave about their rainbow cookies). Pelham Bay Park is a great place to see how beautiful and diverse the Bronx landscape really is.

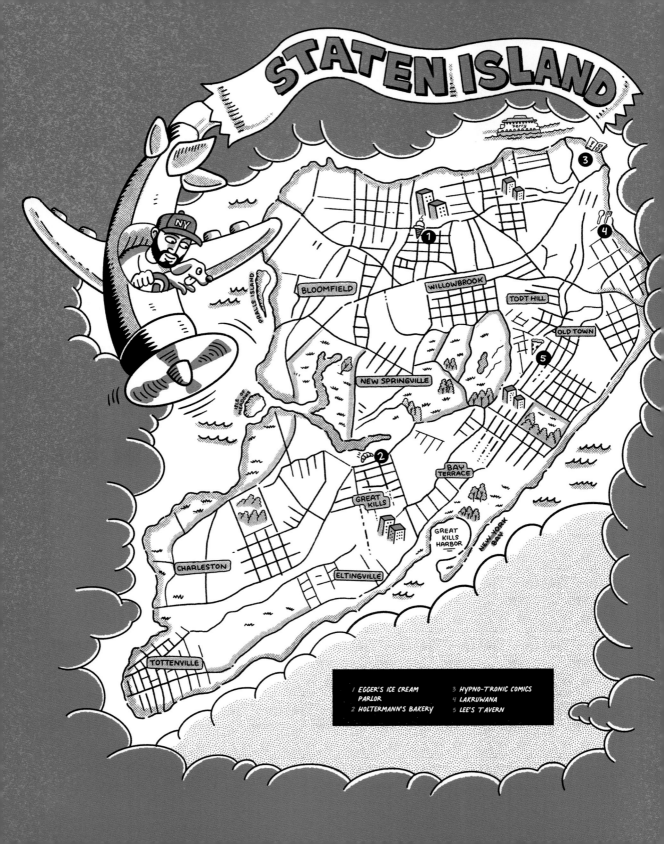

Staten Island unfairly gets relegated to some sort of "fifth borough" status or a punch line in a joke. The borough can be hard to get to know. It's a little challenging to access and less showy than its neighbors. You need to take a ferry or cross the Verrazzano-Narrows Bridge to get there. It doesn't have the showstopping skyscrapers, Broadway shows, the Knicks, Yankees, or Mets. For me, that's what makes it so appealing. Staten Island is a world unto itself. It puts its own twist on NYC culture. You can't truly know NYC without visiting all five boroughs, and Staten Island is as important to the story as anywhere else.

Staten Island is also the home of my friend Cugine. Few rep SI harder than Cug. There's a good chance you've seen a video of him making a chicken parm while talking about "ya sistah" or extolling the virtues of Diet Coke. Cug is the person I message when I need a Staten rec. Part of the reason Cug has become so well-known is his charm, and part of that charm comes from the fact that he *sounds* like Staten Island. Listen closely and you start to notice how NYC accents vary from borough to borough.

The easiest way to get to Staten Island is on the legendary Staten Island Ferry. It's a beautiful twenty-five-minute boat ride that passes the Statue of Liberty. It's also free. That's ample reason for people to check out the home of Wu-Tang Clan and Pete Davidson. Staten Island has the smallest population of all five boroughs, but it's the third largest in terms of landmass, so it's good to have a plan before going. This section should help you navigate.

Once you get there, you'll find some of the best Sri Lankan food in the city, the Staten Island Zoo, the oldest cricket club in the country, and one of the best clam pizzas anywhere. That alone should make you want to get on the ferry and check it out.

EGGER'S ICE CREAM PARLOR

1194 FOREST AVENUE

ou ever watch old black-and-white movies showing teens hanging out in an old-school soda shop? There's always one with a New York accent, usually the tough guy. You can still see a few vestiges of that past when you go to places in Manhattan like Lexington Candy Shop (page 52), but for the most part those old-timey soda shops are gone. Egger's Ice Cream Parlor might be the closest to the original I've found. Operating since 1932, it's a place generations of Staten Island locals have fond memories of, including my friend Cugine. The first time he took me there, it

felt like I was hanging out with Little Cug. He seemed excited to be back in a place he went to as a child, along with this family.

Egger's was founded by German-born baker Richie Egger. In 2014, lifelong Staten Island resident Danielle Raleigh took over operations. Her business plan was simple: to keep things the way they've been since the old days (with a couple of modern touches, of course). You still walk up to the long counter lined with stools and order anything from a sundae to a simple cup of cherry vanilla or mint chocolate chip ice cream. You can still get a malted milkshake made

Every December, they have their Egger's Winter Wonderland event in Snug Harbor, where you can eat ice cream and drink hot cocoa in private heated igloos, and even meet the Staten Island Santa Claus.

the old-fashioned way, and the smell of hot fudge deliciously permeates the air. Danielle knew she had to add a few new things to keep up with the times. Vegan ice cream wasn't something you saw along Forest Avenue too often until Egger's started serving it. Now it's a huge seller.

But what makes Egger's stand out is how very New York it feels, but more specifically, very Staten Island. There aren't many places in all of New York City I'd describe as "quaint," but that's the best word I can think of. I like going to Egger's because they have the best ice cream in their neck of the woods, and because it's nice to reconnect with the way we used to do things. It's a way that feels natural—too bad we don't do it more often. Just people hanging out at the ice cream parlor; that's pretty nice.

HOLTERMANN'S BAKERY

405 ARTHUR KILL ROAD

Everything here is old school. I'd say most of the machines are from the 1930s, and we weigh everything out ourselves," Jill Holtermann Bowers tells me as we walk through the cavernous bakery her family founded in 1878. Jill's a fourth-generation owner. She grew up working at the bakery, then became a teacher for a little while, but the bakery called her back. "When I was a kid, when Christmas came, all the kids in the family would stand around this big wooden work bench. We all got trays of cookies, the boxes would go around, and you'd have to fill the boxes. And at the end, Grandpa Holtermann would say, 'Okay, you can have *one* cookie.'"

Now she can have all the cookies she wants. And her bakery has plenty of them. Butter cookies, black-and-whites, gingerbread, you name it, they make it. They also have pies, bread, cakes, and macaroons.

The buttered roll. A New York icon. IYKYK. Jill says she's proud of how perfect the rolls at Holtermann's are, so you've gotta stop in for breakfast and try one.

TIP

"I've got this massive box with my great-grandpa Holtermann's recipes. It's all been handed down through the generations," Jill says.

One thing that came along with the recipes is the attention to making everything just right. "We do all this stuff by hand," Jill says as she shows us some of the birthday cakes going out that afternoon. Same with the cupcakes and donuts and anything with a glaze. It's something we all sometimes take for granted these days. We forget how much work and passion goes into some of the things we eat. And at a place like Holtermann's, combine that passion along with the many years the family has been serving the community, and you get an experience unlike anywhere else. Jill is proud of the work she's continuing, and as she keeps handing me sweets to sample as we walk through the bakery, I can understand why.

STATEN ISLAND

207

HYPNO-TRONIC COMICS

156 STUYVESANT PLACE

Some people just decide they have a calling. Joy Ghigliotti was always into comics, but owning a comic book store wasn't what she started out doing.

"I was a social worker before I opened," Joy says. She was already helping people, but there was something else she wanted to do. Being a social worker can be a rewarding job, but it's also extremely challenging and emotionally taxing. But so can being a comic book shop owner. She tells me the story from her seat behind the counter of Staten Island's best, and only, comic book shop. "There was another one when I opened that was pretty cool, but

it closed. Then there was another one that was around until [Hurricane] Sandy took it out."

If there's going to be a single comic book shop for an entire borough, it needs to be a cathedral to all things new and vintage comics, toys, Marvel, DC, big names, unknown ones. I get on the ferry just to come here because I know I'll find whatever I'm looking for, and at least two or three things I've never heard of. That doesn't happen as much in Manhattan or Brooklyn, where space is at such a premium that shop owners are forced to make room for new products.

I can't imagine not having a comic shop around me at any point in my life.

I'm spoiled because I grew up in NYC, but Staten Island is still only a boat ride away, and it's easy to see how important a place like this is for kids who want something more than just the same TV shows and video games.

"We've got everything," Joy says. And when she says that, she means they've got all the superhero stuff, but there's also something for everybody obsessed with the odd, grotesque, colorful, strange, and funny. "We wanted to be like Love Saves the Day," she says.

I think that's really cool. Love Saves the Day was this great old vintage shop on the corner of Seventh Street and Second Avenue that catered to East Village weirdos. While it was geared more toward the fashion-minded than Hypno-Tronic Comics is, I can see the connection. Joy has made a space for people who love comics, but it's also welcoming to people who might not know much beyond Batman and Captain America. Everybody who visits finds something they like.

TIP

There are so many museums in New York City that you're bound to overlook one or a dozen. A great one is a few minutes' walk from Hypno-Tronic, the National Lighthouse Museum. It's small, but you'll know more about lighthouses than just about anybody else if you visit.

LAKRUWANA

668 BAY STREET

Staten Island might be best known for Wu-Tang Clan, Pete Davidson, and, of course, Meals by Cug, but it's also home to one of the largest populations of Sri Lankans outside the South Asian country itself.

"It's a small island, so having three thousand people from there on Staten Island is crazy," Julia Wijesinghe of Lakruwana says.

"This is a family business, so it's hard to say what my title is since I was born into it," Julia tells me with a smile. Her family opened the original Sri Lankan spot in Manhattan in 1995 before moving to Staten Island to be closer to the large community of immigrants from their home country.

Julia and her family are pioneers when it comes to Sri Lankan cooking in the city. That's why people have no issue hopping on the ferry over to Staten Island because they know the food served at Lakruwana is unlike anything else they can get anywhere else in the city. Lakruwana also doesn't look like anywhere else. The decor is incredible. The entire experience is unique.

"We always get compared with Indian food since we're both curry-

TIP

Julia opened the Sri Lankan
Art and Cultural Museum
a few blocks away, at
61 Canal Street, when she
was just eighteen, making
her the youngest museum
owner in the world. It was
originally in the basement of
the restaurant, but she moved
it to its current space with a
mission to share the vibrant
arts and cultural scene of Sri
Lanka. That's pretty impressive
and you should check it out.

based," she says, "but the difference is we use coconut milk. Everything has it. Without coconut, it's hard to make a Sri Lankan dish."

When I ask for a recommendation, Julia doesn't hesitate: The first thing to order is the lamprais. A dish with origins over three hundred years old, it's the protein of your choice wrapped in a banana leaf with egg, basmati rice, eggplant, and more. I got mine with chicken, and asked for it moderately spicy, and the flavors and aromas when it

hit the table were different from anything I've ever experienced. I also got an order of chicken hoppers, which are crispy oval-shaped pancakes, and, of course, I tried their roti. It was incredible.

You can eat a lot at Lakruwana if you're not from Staten Island, because once you're done, you go outside, take a little walk to work off the food, and then you get on a boat to get home. It's New York City's "dinner and a cruise."

LEE'S TAVERN

60 HANCOCK STREET

At some point in the last decade or so, the rest of the world started hearing about white clam pizza. You can thank New Haven, Connecticut, for that, not New York. And all due respect to our neighbors, but it's a little weird that people would go that wild for pizza from a place nicknamed the Nutmeg State. So I figured that somewhere in the five boroughs there had to be a great pizza topped with clams. Thankfully, I've got a guy who knows all about this stuff. I asked my pal Cugine, and he said that clam pies have been eaten by locals at the old wooden bar at Lee's Tavern on Staten Island since 1940.

When I asked Cugine if there was anything besides the pizza he goes there for, he answered, "What, are you kidding?

The buffalo calamari at Lee's is necessary. It pairs well with the garlic bread they make. Get it with the mozzarella baked on top. Delicious.

Fucking calamari in the hot marinara sauce, and then *at least* one of the *two* clam pies," since they have both red and white versions. Another must-order on the menu is the shredded pork with onions and peppers—that's the suggestion of third-generation (second in his family) owner, Diego Palemine.

What you notice right away when you walk into Lee's is that it's old school and charming in a very organic way. Natural light beams in through the windows, spotlighting a cozy interior that feels untouched by

time. Diego's father bought the place from its original owner in 1969. There are plaques for local Little League teams that the bar supports, trophies from Diego's hunting excursions, and a proud painting of the elder Palemine, Dickie. It feels like a members-only club that welcomes anybody so long as they like good pizza.

"My dad worked here as a kid. He grew up a few blocks away and dad had a few jobs before this. He was a mailman. He wanted to join the police force, but he had screws in his ankles so he couldn't be a cop. Then in sixty-nine, Lee wanted to retire and he sold it to my dad with the stipulations that he keep the name and that Mr. Lee could work whenever he wanted."

Diego doesn't like to give away the secret ingredients in the homemade sauce, but when I take a bite, there's this rush of fresh garlic and oregano. Something like clams can often overpower any dish, but that's not the case with the pizza at Lee's Tavern. The flavor is balanced because they figured out that when you hit on something good, you shouldn't mess with it.

"Why try to complicate things? I went to culinary school, and they were telling me I should do this and do that, and I just didn't understand why," Diego says. "Everybody is trying to turn pizza into a gourmet meal and at the end of the day it's still just a pizza." What matters is whether it's great or not, and the pizza at Lee's Tavern is very much worth the trip.

MANHATTAN

- [ ] **ABRACADABRA**
19 West 21st Street, 2

- [ ] **ALBANESE MEATS & POULTRY**
238 Elizabeth Street, 4

- [ ] **ARMY & NAVY BAGS**
177 East Houston Street #2, 6

- [ ] **ASTOR PLACE HAIRSTYLISTS**
740 Broadway, 2 Astor Place, 8

- [ ] **B&H DAIRY**
127 Second Avenue, 12

- [ ] **BALLOON SALOON**
133 West Broadway, 14

- [ ] **BAZ BAGEL**
181 Grand Street, 16

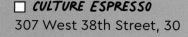

- [ ] **CAFFÈ PANNA**
77 Irving Place, 18

- [ ] **CASA ADELA**
66 Loisaida Avenue, 20

- [ ] **CASA MAGAZINES**
22 Eighth Avenue, 22

- [ ] **CASEY RUBBER STAMPS**
322 East 11th Street, 24

- [ ] **CHESS FORUM**
219 Thompson Street, 26

- [ ] **COZY SOUP 'N' BURGER**
739 Broadway, 28

- [ ] **CULTURE ESPRESSO**
307 West 38th Street, 30

- [ ] **E.ROSSI & COMPANY**
193 Grand Street, 32

- [ ] **ECONOMY CANDY**
108 Rivington Street, 34

- [ ] **FISHS EDDY**
889 Broadway, 36

- [ ] **GRANDMA'S PLACE**
84 West 120th Street, 38

- [ ] **GREENWICH LOCKSMITHS**
56 Seventh Avenue South, 40

- [ ] **THE HOT DOG KING**
Fifth Avenue & East 82nd Street,
in front of the Metropolitan
Museum of Art, 42

- [ ] **KATZ'S DELICATESSEN**
205 East Houston Street, 44

- [ ] **LA BONBONNIERE**
28 Eighth Avenue, 46

- [ ] **LA SIRENA MEXICAN FOLK ART**
27 East 3rd Street, 48

- [ ] **LEE LEE'S BAKED GOODS**
283 West 118th Street, 50

- [ ] **LEXINGTON CANDY SHOP**
1226 Lexington Avenue, 52

- [ ] **MAMA'S TOO!**
2750 Broadway, 54

- [ ] **MERCER STREET BOOKS**
206 Mercer Street, 56

- [ ] **MR. THROWBACK**
437 East 9th Street, 58

- [ ] **MUSIC INN WORLD INSTRUMENTS**
  169 West 4th Street, 60

- [ ] **MYZEL'S CHOCOLATES**
  140 West 55th Street #1, 62

- [ ] **ORO LATINO JEWELRY**
  82 Bowery, 64

- [ ] **PAGEANT PRINT SHOP**
  69 East 4th Street, 66

- [ ] **PEARL RIVER MART**
  452 Broadway, 68

- [ ] **PUNJABI DELI**
  114 East 1st Street, 70

- [ ] **RAY'S CANDY STORE**
  113 Avenue A, 72

- [ ] **ROGUE**
  154 Allen Street, 74

- [ ] **RUSS & DAUGHTERS**
  179 East Houston Street, 76

- [ ] **S&P LUNCH**
  174 Fifth Avenue, 78

- [ ] **SWEET PICKLE BOOKS**
  47 Orchard Street, 80

- [ ] **THE SOCK MAN**
  99 St. Marks Place, 82

- [ ] **TING'S GIFT SHOP**
  18 Doyers Street, 84

- [ ] **TOY TOKYO**
  91 Second Avenue, 86

- [ ] **VESELKA**
  144 Second Avenue, 88

- [ ] **VILLAGE REVIVAL RECORDS**
  197 Bleecker Street, 90

- [ ] **VILLAGE WORKS**
  12 St. Marks Place, 92

- [ ] **YU & ME BOOKS**
  44 Mulberry Street, 94

BROOKLYN

- [ ] **ALLAN'S BAKERY**
  1109 Nostrand Avenue, 98

- [ ] **ANTHONY & SON PANINI SHOPPE**
  433 Graham Avenue, 100

- [ ] **THE BAKERY ON BERGEN**
  740 Bergen Street, 104

- [ ] **BULLETPROOF COMICS**
  2178 Nostrand Avenue, 106

- [ ] **CIRCO'S PASTRY SHOP**
  312 Knickerbocker Avenue, 108

- [ ] **CLOUDY DONUT**
  14 Columbia Place, 110

- [ ] **CREST HARDWARE & URBAN GARDEN CENTER**
  558 Metropolitan Avenue, 112

- [ ] **CUTS & SLICES**
  93 Howard Avenue, 114

☐ **DEFONTE'S SANDWICH SHOP**
379 Columbia Street, 116

☐ **FANTASY EXPLOSION**
164A Driggs Avenue, 118

☐ **5TH AVENUE RECORDS**
439 Fifth Avenue, 120

☐ **FORTUNATO BROTHERS**
289 Manhattan Avenue, 122

☐ **GREENBERG'S BAGELS**
1065 Bedford Avenue, 124

☐ **L'INDUSTRIE PIZZERIA**
254 S 2nd Street, 126

☐ **LUIGI'S PIZZA**
686 Fifth Avenue, 128

☐ **NENES TAQUERIA**
14 Starr Street, 130

☐ **PEPPA'S JERK CHICKEN**
738 Flatbush Avenue, 132

☐ **PETER PAN DONUT & PASTRY SHOP**
727 Manhattan Avenue, 134

☐ **POP'S POPULAR CLOTHING**
7 Franklin Street, 136

☐ **QUIMBY'S BOOKSTORE**
536 Metropolitan Avenue, 138

☐ **SACRED VIBES APOTHECARY**
376 Argyle Road, 140

☐ **SETTEPANI BAKERY**
602 Lorimer Street, 142

☐ **TAQUERIA RAMIREZ**
94 Franklin Street, 144

☐ **VILLABATE ALBA**
7001 18th Avenue, 146

☐ **YESTERDAY'S NEWS ANTIQUES & COLLECTIBLES**
428 Court Street, 148

QUEENS

☐ **COMFORTLAND**
40–09 30th Avenue, 152

☐ **FUSKAHOUSE**
7301 37th Avenue, 154

☐ **THE LEMON ICE KING OF CORONA**
52–02 108th Street, 156

☐ **LOUIE'S PIZZA**
81–34 Baxter Avenue #1, 158

☐ **NEIR'S TAVERN**
87–48 78th Street, 160

☐ **NEPALI BHANCHHA GHAR**
74–15 Roosevelt Avenue, 162

☐ **PHO METRO**
31–16 Farrington Street, 164

☐ **RUDY'S HOBBY & ART**
35–16 30th Avenue, 166

☐ **SUPER BURRITO**
190 Beach 69th Street, 168

☐ **TRINCITI ROTI SHOP**
111–03 Lefferts Boulevard, 170

☐ **UTOPIA BAGELS**
1909 Utopia Parkway, 172

THE BRONX

- [ ] *188 CUCHIFRITOS*
  158 East 188th Street, 176

- [ ] *AJO Y OREGANO*
  621 Crescent Avenue, 178

- [ ] *BRONX NATIVE*
  127 Lincoln Avenue, 180

- [ ] *CASA AMADEO*
  786 Prospect Avenue, 182

- [ ] *CONTI'S PASTRY SHOPPE*
  786 Morris Park Avenue, 184

- [ ] *DAN'S PARENTS' HOUSE*
  239 City Island Avenue, 186

- [ ] *JOHNNY'S REEF*
  2 City Island Avenue, 188

- [ ] *LIEBMAN'S DELI*
  552 West 235th Street, 190

- [ ] *LLOYD'S CARROT CAKE*
  6087 Broadway, 192

- [ ] *LOUIE & ERNIE'S PIZZA*
  1300 Crosby Avenue, 194

- [ ] *MIKE'S DELI*
  2344 Arthur Avenue, 196

- [ ] *TAKOUT*
  2435 Grand Concourse, 198

- [ ] *THIRD EYE THROWBACKS*
  3004 Middletown Road, 200

STATEN ISLAND

- [ ] *EGGER'S ICE CREAM PARLOR*
  1194 Forest Avenue, 204

- [ ] *HOLTERMANN'S BAKERY*
  405 Arthur Kill Road, 206

- [ ] *HYPNO-TRONIC COMICS*
  156 Stuyvesant Place, 208

- [ ] *LAKRUWANA*
  668 Bay Street, 210

- [ ] *LEE'S TAVERN*
  60 Hancock Street, 212

ACKNOWLEDGMENTS

THANK YOU TO:

Jason Diamond, Jeremy Cohen, Jessica Flores,
Stuart Roberts, Dan Milaschewski, Meredith Miller,
Isaiah Telewoda, Sarah Mathews, Christopher Wilson,
Ploy Siripant, Naomi Otsu, Kasey Feather,
Allison Carney, Heidi Richter, Renata De Oliveira,
Carrie Thornton, and every single person featured
in this book.

ew York Nico (Nicolas Heller) is a filmmaker and social media creator born and raised in NYC. Hailed by the *New York Times* as the "unofficial talent scout of NYC," New York Nico documents New York City for his nearly three million followers across his platforms.

He has directed commercial campaigns for the New York Knicks, Meta, NIKE, MLB, Calvin Klein, Kith, Timberland, and his last film, *Out of Order*, premiered at the Tribeca Film Festival.

He frequently uses his platform to highlight small businesses that make up the fabric of their communities. During the COVID-19 pandemic, he used his videos to help raise money to keep several at-risk shops in business.

President Joe Biden recognized his work by presenting him with the President's Lifetime Achievement Award in 2021.

DEYST.

NEW YORK NICO'S GUIDE TO NYC. Copyright © 2024 by Heller Media Ltd. All rights reserved. Printed in Canada. No part of this book may be used or reproduced in any manner whatsoever without written permission except in the case of brief quotations embodied in critical articles and reviews. For information, address HarperCollins Publishers, 195 Broadway, New York, NY 10007.

HarperCollins books may be purchased for educational, business, or sales promotional use. For information, please email the Special Markets Department at SPsales@harpercollins.com.

FIRST EDITION

DESIGNED BY RENATA DE OLIVEIRA

Photographs by Jeremy Cohen
Produced by Jessica Flores

Library of Congress Cataloging-in-Publication Data has been applied for.

ISBN 978-0-06-331979-0

24 25 26 27 28 TC 5 4 3 2 1